Midwest Living®

TASTE OF THE SEASONS

Meredith® Consumer Marketing
Des Moines, Iowa

Midwest Living® Taste of the Seasons

Meredith® Corporation Consumer Marketing
VICE PRESIDENT, CONSUMER MARKETING: Janet Donnelly
CONSUMER MARKETING PRODUCT DIRECTOR: Heather Sorensen
BUSINESS DIRECTOR: Ron Clingman
CONSUMER MARKETING PRODUCT MANAGER: Wendy Merical
SENIOR PRODUCTION MANAGER: Al Rodruck

Waterbury Publications, Inc.
EDITORIAL DIRECTOR: Lisa Kingsley
ASSOCIATE EDITORS: Tricia Bergman, Mary Williams
CREATIVE DIRECTOR: Ken Carlson
ASSOCIATE DESIGN DIRECTOR: Doug Samuelson
PRODUCTION ASSISTANT: Mindy Samuelson
CONTRIBUTING COPY EDITORS: Terri Fredrickson, Linda Wagner
CONTRIBUTING INDEXER: Elizabeth T. Parson

***Midwest Living*® Magazine**
EDITOR IN CHIEF: Greg Philby
CREATIVE DIRECTOR: Geri Wolfe Boesen
EXECUTIVE EDITOR: Trevor Meers
FOOD EDITOR: Hannah Agran
COPY CHIEF: Maria Duryée

Meredith National Media Group
PRESIDENT: Tom Harty

Meredith Corporation
PRESIDENT AND CHIEF EXECUTIVE OFFICER: Stephen M. Lacy

IN MEMORIAM: E.T. Meredith III (1933–2003)

Pictured on the front cover:
Peanut Butter Buckeye Brownie Cheesecake
(recipe on page 177)
Photographer: Pete Krumhardt

All of us at Meredith® Corporation Consumer Marketing are dedicated to providing you with information and ideas to enhance your home. We welcome your comments and suggestions. Write to us at: Meredith Consumer Marketing, 1716 Locust St., Des Moines, IA 50309-3023.

Contents

The Starting Plate

LAKE VACATIONS OFFICIALLY BEGIN WHEN, like the clang of an opening bell, a resort's worn, heat-scorched, chipped-handled pot is pulled out of the cupboard and set upon the cabin's cooktop. Sure, there are other signs of arrival, such as the first heady trek to the shore to survey the possibilities lapping and rippling out almost endlessly. There's the bang of the cabin door and the unpacking of bags. But none pronounce the sense of arrival like the first meal.

My family tradition is to heat up chili, bringing it frozen and letting it thaw and bubble as we set up our new home for the week. It's simple and efficient, and it is also gratifyingly grounding—anointing the cabin, if you will, with a sense of *us*. Even though it's the same family-favorite chili that carries us through the cold season (see the Winter chapter for several great chili options), it plays a different role here, coming along as a warm family friend.

All of you, too, have foods that carry significance, whether related to a vacation or a holiday or connected to a change in the Midwest seasons. In this collection of *Taste of the Seasons*, we package the wonderful flavors we gathered during the past year. Our Test Kitchen makes sure they are all easy and reliable; we editors make sure they taste really, really good.

As the chili gurgles in the beat-up pot, my family takes its place within the community of all those who have used the pot before, joining a decades-deep culinary kinship. But we also celebrate something more tightly knit: a sense of family, a sense of place, and a special food to bring it all together. This book has many such foods. Explore them, enjoy them, and create your own sense of arrival, even if it is just around your dining room table.

GregPhilby
Editor in Chief

SPRING PASTA WITH
MORELS, RAMPS
AND PEAS, PAGE 33

Spring

APPETIZERS
Arugula Pesto 22
Asparagus Fritters 21
Herbed Deviled Egg Bruschetta 21
Napa Cabbage Spring Rolls 18
Pea-Shoot Soup 24
Spring Greens Soup 24

BREADS
Overnight Pull-Apart Cinnamon Loaf 14

BREAKFAST
Breakfast Burritos 11
English Muffin and Asparagus Bake 12
Omelet with Morel Cream Sauce 12
Strawberry-Rhubarb Freezer Jam 9

MAIN DISHES
Crisp Portobello Mushroom and Spring Carrot Salad 36
Ham-and-Asparagus-Stuffed Chicken 31
Ham and Pea Soup 27
Herbed Cheese-Stuffed Salmon 31
Honey Roast Chicken with Spring Peas and Shallots 28
Morel and Asparagus Crispy Pizza 33
Sesame Pork and Noodles 27
Soba Noodle Bowl 28
Spring Chicken Stew 27
Spring Pasta with Morels, Ramps and Peas 33

SIDES
Napa Cabbage and Black Bean Slaw 36
Red Potato Salad with Mustard Dressing 39
Sweet Curry Carrots with Chive Yogurt 39

SWEETS
Blueberry-Rhubarb Cobbler 43
Cream-Filled Cannoli 51
Irresistible Tiramisu 48
Just-Right Rhubarb Pie 40
Lemon-Rosemary Cheesecake 48
Meringue with Seared Pineapple 44
Pineapple Upside-Down Cake 47

Strawberry-Rhubarb Freezer Jam

Strawberries and rhubarb are a sweet-tart odd couple to be sure—but then, Mother Nature always was an excellent matchmaker. Redder rhubarb is often sweeter, but every stalk varies. Keep the sugar bowl close and sweeten to taste.

PREP 35 minutes **STAND** 24 hours

  3 cups strawberries
  1 cup finely chopped fresh rhubarb
  5 cups sugar
  ½ teaspoon lemon zest
  ¾ cup water
  1 1.75-ounce package regular powdered fruit
    pectin

1. In a large bowl, use potato masher to crush berries. You'll have about 1½ cups. Stir in rhubarb. Stir in sugar and lemon zest. Let stand 10 minutes, stirring occasionally. In a small saucepan, mix the water and pectin. Bring to boiling over high heat; boil 1 minute, stirring constantly. Remove from heat; add to berry mixture. Stir 3 minutes or until sugar dissolves and mixture is not grainy.

2. Ladle into half-pint freezer containers, leaving ½-inch headspace. Seal and label. Let stand at room temperature 24 hours until set. Store 3 weeks in refrigerator or up to 1 year in freezer. **Makes 5 half-pints.**

Per tablespoon: 53 cal, 0 g fat, 0 mg chol, 1 mg sodium, 14 g carbo, 0 g fiber, 0 g pro.

Freezer jam couldn't be simpler to make, and the rewards are sweet. At breakfast on a January morning, this jam offers a taste of the spring that was—and the one to come.

Breakfast Burritos

PREP 20 minutes **COOK** 25 minutes

6 10-inch flour or whole wheat flour tortillas
1 tablespoon butter or margarine
1 cup refrigerated shredded hash brown potatoes
½ cup cooked breakfast sausage, bulk pork sausage, cooked bulk turkey sausage, diced Canadian-style bacon or diced cooked ham
2 slices bacon, crisp-cooked, drained and crumbled
6 eggs
⅓ cup milk
¼ teaspoon salt
¼ teaspoon chili powder or freshly ground black pepper
1 tablespoon butter or margarine
¼ cup chopped onion
¼ cup finely chopped green or red sweet pepper
1 4.5-ounce can diced green chile peppers, drained
¾ cup crumbled queso fresco, shredded Monterey Jack cheese or shredded cheddar cheese (3 ounces)
⅓ cup sour cream
⅓ cup red and/or green chunky salsa
Snipped fresh cilantro (optional)
Red and/or green chunky salsa (optional)

1. Stack and wrap tortillas in foil; heat in a 350° oven for 10 minutes or until heated through. (Or wrap in paper towels and microwave on 100% power [high] about 1 minute or until heated through.)

2. In a medium nonstick skillet, melt the 1 tablespoon butter over medium heat. Stir in potatoes. Spread in an even layer; press down lightly with spatula. Cook 6 to 7 minutes or until golden brown on the bottom. Flip potatoes with a spatula. Cook 6 to 8 minutes more or until golden brown and crisp (turn as necessary for even browning). Stir in sausage and bacon; heat through. Remove from heat; keep warm.

3. In a small bowl, whisk eggs, milk, salt and chili powder. In a large skillet, melt 1 tablespoon butter over medium heat; add onion and sweet pepper. Cook over medium heat until vegetables are tender. Pour in egg mixture. Cook over medium heat, without stirring, until mixture begins to set on bottom and around edges.

4. With a spatula, lift and fold the partially cooked egg mixture so the uncooked portion flows underneath. Continue cooking and folding for 2 to 3 minutes or until egg mixture is cooked through but still glossy and moist. Immediately remove from heat.

5. Divide potato mixture evenly among tortillas, placing just below center. Top each with some of the egg mixture, green chile peppers, cheese, sour cream and the ⅓ cup salsa. Fold each tortilla into a burrito. If you like, garnish with cilantro and serve with additional salsa. **Makes 6 burritos.**

Per burrito: 465 cal, 23 g fat, 238 mg chol, 1,135 mg sodium, 45 g carbo, 4 g fiber, 20 g pro.

These hearty burritos take all of the elements of a restaurant-style breakfast platter—eggs, sausage, bacon, and hash brown potatoes—and wrap them up in a portable nosh flavored with salsa, Mexican cheese and chilies.

English Muffin and Asparagus Bake

PREP 25 minutes   **BAKE** 12 minutes
BROIL 2 minutes

  1 orange, yellow or green sweet pepper
10 eggs
½ cup half-and-half or milk
  2 teaspoons Dijon-style mustard
  1 teaspoon lemon pepper seasoning
  1 teaspoon curry powder
¼ teaspoon salt
  1 tablespoon olive oil
  6 to 8 ounces thin asparagus spears, trimmed
  1 cup fresh sugar snap pea pods, trimmed
  1 cup red or yellow cherry tomatoes
  2 English muffins, split and halved
  4 ounces fresh mozzarella cheese, thinly
      sliced, or 1 cup shredded mozzarella
¼ cup fresh basil leaves

1. Slice bottom half of pepper into rings; seed and chop remaining pepper half. Set aside.

2. In a large bowl, whisk together eggs, half-and-half, mustard, lemon pepper, curry powder and salt; set aside.

3. In a 12-inch nonstick oven-going skillet, heat oil over medium heat. Add asparagus spears; cook 1 to 2 minutes or until bright green. Remove and set aside. Add chopped sweet pepper and pea pods; cook 2 minutes. Stir in tomatoes. Cook until tomato skins begin to pop. Cut each muffin half into 2 pieces. Arrange muffin pieces on vegetables. Pour egg mixture over all. Top with asparagus, pressing lightly.

4. Bake, uncovered, in a 350°F oven for 12 minutes. Top with pepper rings and cheese. Turn oven to broil. Broil 2 to 3 minutes or until eggs are set.

5. Loosen edges and slide onto serving platter. Cut in wedges. Top with fresh basil leaves. **Makes 6 servings.**

Per serving: 293 cal, 18 g fat, 375 mg chol, 525 mg sodium, 16 g carbo, 2 g fiber, 18 g pro.

Omelet with Morel Cream Sauce

Remember this sauce when you need a delicious topping for chicken, fish or steak.

START TO FINISH 35 minutes

10 ounces fresh morel mushrooms, cleaned
      and sliced ¼ inch thick
  1 tablespoon butter
¼ cup finely chopped red onion
½ teaspoon cracked black pepper
  2 tablespoons brandy (optional)
  1 cup whipping cream
¼ cup reduced-sodium chicken stock or broth
  2 cups shredded spinach
  2 teaspoons snipped fresh tarragon or basil
  4 ounces shredded Swiss cheese (1 cup)
  8 eggs
  4 tablespoons water
      Salt and black pepper
  4 to 8 teaspoons butter

1. For sauce: In a large skillet, cook and stir morels in hot butter over medium-high heat for 3 minutes. Add onion and pepper; cook for 2 minutes. Remove skillet from heat; add brandy, if you like. Return to heat and cook for 1 minute. Add cream and stock; cook and stir for 6 to 8 minutes or until slightly thickened.

2. Reduce heat to low. Cook until sauce is very thick. Remove from heat, stir in spinach and tarragon. Cool sauce slightly, then stir in the shredded Swiss cheese.

3. Meanwhile, for each omelet: Beat 2 eggs and 1 tablespoon of the water in a small bowl; season to taste with salt and pepper. Heat 1 to 2 teaspoons butter in a medium nonstick skillet over medium-high heat until bubbling. Pour in egg mixture. Push cooked portion to center of skillet, tilting the skillet so uncooked egg fills skillet. When no liquid egg remains, place one-fourth of the sauce on one side of omelet and fold other side over filling. Transfer to serving plate. **Makes 4 omelets.**

Per serving: 542 cal, 47 g fat, 549 mg chol, 899 mg sodium, 8 g carbo, 1 g fiber, 24 g pro.

OMELET WITH MOREL
CREAM SAUCE

Overnight Pull-Apart Cinnamon Loaf

This no-knead dough is made the day before and allowed to rise overnight in the fridge to develop flavor.

PREP 30 minutes **RISE** overnight + 45 minutes **BAKE** 30 minutes **COOL** 30 minutes

¾ cup milk
1 package active dry yeast
¼ cup butter, melted
2 tablespoons granulated sugar
1 egg, lightly beaten
½ teaspoon salt
3 cups all-purpose flour
¼ cup butter, melted
¾ cup granulated sugar
2 teaspoons ground cinnamon
Quick Glaze (recipe follows)
Chopped pistachio nuts (optional)

1. In a small saucepan, heat milk just until warm (105° to 115°). Pour into a large mixing bowl, then add the yeast. Stir until yeast is dissolved. Let stand 5 minutes or until foamy.

2. With a mixer, beat ¼ cup melted butter, 2 tablespoons sugar, egg and salt into the yeast mixture until combined. Add half the flour, then beat on low speed for 30 seconds, scraping bowl as needed. Increase speed to medium and beat 3 minutes more. Stir in remaining flour. Shape in a ball (dough will not be smooth). Transfer to an oiled bowl. Cover and refrigerate overnight. (Or, to make right away, cover and set aside in a warm place to rise 45 to 60 minutes or until nearly double.)

3. Butter a 9x5x3-inch loaf pan; set aside. Remove dough from refrigerator. On lightly floured surface, roll dough to 20x12-inch rectangle. Brush with ¼ cup melted butter and sprinkle with a mixture of ¾ cup sugar and the cinnamon. Cut dough rectangle crosswise in five 12x4-inch strips. Stack strips, then cut six 4x2-inch pieces. Loosely stagger the stacks in the prepared pan, cut sides up.

4. Let rise in a warm place 45 minutes or until nearly double in size. Preheat oven to 350°. Bake loaf 30 minutes or until golden brown. Cool in pan on wire rack for 10 minutes. Remove from pan and transfer to serving plate. Drizzle with Quick Glaze and sprinkle with nuts if desired. Cool 20 minutes more. Pull apart slices or slice to serve. **Makes 12 servings.**

Quick Glaze: In a small bowl, stir together 1 cup powdered sugar, ½ teaspoon vanilla and 1 to 2 tablespoons milk for drizzling consistency.

Per serving: 296 cal, 9 g fat, 37 mg chol, 180 mg sodium, 50 g carbo, 1 g fiber, 5 g pro.

You don't need special gear or skills to see migrant birds. All you need is a day to slow down and speak quietly as you step into nature's springtime embrace.

The spring thaw swells creeks that tumble over rocky ledges. At Gooseberry Falls State Park in Minnesota, visitors experience the thunderous roar of the Upper, Middle and Lower falls of the Gooseberry River as it plummets through a rocky gorge. Catch the beautiful views of the Lake Superior shoreline and sightings of North Woods wildlife.

Napa Cabbage Spring Rolls

Spring rolls are a great way to let the flavors of fresh vegetables shine.

PREP 25 minutes **COOK** 15 minutes **STAND** 1 hour

½ cup Arborio rice or long grain rice
1 tablespoon sea salt or kosher salt
4 cups ice cubes
1 head Napa cabbage or savoy cabbage
1 cup shredded or grated carrots
½ cup finely chopped green onions
2 tablespoons snipped fresh Italian
    (flat-leaf) parsley
1 tablespoon sesame oil (not toasted)
¼ teaspoon lime zest
2 teaspoons lime juice
½ teaspoon sea salt or kosher salt
¼ teaspoon freshly ground black pepper
    Soy sauce* or teriyaki sauce

1. In a medium saucepan, bring 1 cup water to boiling. Slowly add rice and return to boiling; reduce heat. Simmer, covered, 15 minutes or until most of the water is absorbed and the rice is tender. Remove from heat. Let stand, covered, for 5 minutes. Uncover; let rice cool.

2. In a 4- to 5-quart Dutch oven, combine 12 cups (3 quarts) water and the 1 tablespoon sea salt. Bring to boiling. Meanwhile, in a large bowl, combine 8 cups cold water and the ice cubes.

3. Remove 8 outer leaves from cabbage and set the remaining head of cabbage aside. Make a cut through each outer leaf at the base where it attaches to core. Trim off some of the woody stem from these leaves.

4. To blanch, carefully add trimmed cabbage leaves to boiling water; cook for 30 seconds to 1 minute or until just wilted. Cool quickly by plunging leaves into the ice water for 1 minute. Remove leaves from water and lay each flat on a towel to dry.

5. For filling: Finely chop enough of the remaining cabbage to measure 1¾ cups. In a large bowl, combine the finely chopped cabbage, carrots, green onions, parsley, sesame oil, lime zest, lime juice, the ½ teaspoon salt and the pepper.

6. About 1 hour before serving, assemble rolls so the surface of spring rolls has time to dry a little, making them easier to handle. First, squeeze out any excess water from the vegetable filling. On a counter or cutting board, lay a blanched cabbage leaf flat, with stem end toward you. Place ¼ cup of vegetable filling on center of leaf, then place 2 tablespoons of the rice on top of the vegetable mixture.

7. Roll stem end of cabbage leaf over rice and filling. Fold left and right sides over to just cover filling. Continue rolling toward the top of the leaf, wrapping tightly but with care not to tear the leaf. Place finished roll on a serving dish, seam side down. Repeat with remaining leaves, vegetable filling and rice. To serve, if you like, cut each roll in half crosswise on a diagonal to make 16 pieces. Serve with some soy sauce.
Makes 8 spring rolls.

*Tip: To lower sodium, use a reduced-sodium soy sauce for dipping.

Per spring roll: 88 cal, 2 g fat, 0 mg chol, 1,181 mg sodium, 15 g carbo, 2 g fiber, 3 g pro.

These fresh vegetarian spring rolls embody the greenness and lightness of spring. Arborio rice lends a creamy texture to the lime-and-sesame-flavored filling.

HERBED DEVILED EGG
BRUSCHETTA

Herbed Deviled Egg Bruschetta

These toasts are lovely Easter dinner appetizers or serve alongside a salad as a light lunch for four.

START TO FINISH 45 minutes

  4 eggs
  2 tablespoons snipped fresh chives
  1 tablespoon snipped fresh dill
  ¼ cup mayonnaise
  1 tablespoon Dijon-style mustard
  4 slices sandwich bread, toasted
    Salt and black pepper
    Paprika
  2 tablespoons chopped baby dill pickles
  2 tablespoons capers

1. Place eggs in a single layer in a medium saucepan; add water to cover by 1 inch. Bring to rapid boil (large, rapidly breaking bubbles) over high heat. Cover; remove from heat. Let stand 15 minutes. Drain; place in a bowl of ice water until cool enough to handle. Peel immediately under cool running water.

2. In a shallow dish, combine chives and dill. Roll peeled eggs in herbs to coat. Remove eggs to cutting board; slice. Stir mayonnaise and mustard into the remaining herbs.

3. Cut the toast diagonally in half; remove the crust.

4. To serve, spread each toast triangle with some of the Dijon spread and top with egg slices. Sprinkle with salt, pepper and paprika. Serve with chopped baby dill pickles and capers. **Makes 8 appetizer servings.**

Per serving: 123 cal, 8 g fat, 108 mg chol, 412 mg sodium, 7 g carbo, 0 g fiber, 4 g pro.

Asparagus Fritters

PREP 30 minutes **COOK** 3 minutes per batch

  1 pound fresh asparagus spears
  1 tablespoon kosher salt or sea salt
  3 eggs, lightly beaten
  1 cup milk
  1 teaspoon vegetable oil
  2½ cups self-rising flour*
    Vegetable oil for deep-fat frying
    Lemon Garlic Aioli (recipe follows) or honey

1. Wash asparagus. If you like, use a vegetable peeler to scrape scales off asparagus from about halfway down spears. Snap off and discard woody bases. Cut the tips and tender ends into 1-inch lengths. Measure 2 cups; set aside. (Use the remaining less-tender parts in soup or sauces.)

2. In a 4- to 5-quart Dutch oven, combine 6 cups water and the salt. Bring to boiling. Meanwhile, in a large bowl, combine 8 cups cold water with some ice cubes.

3. To blanch, carefully add asparagus pieces to the boiling water; cook for 2 to 3 minutes or until just crisp-tender. Cool quickly by plunging asparagus into the ice water for 1 minute; drain well on several layers of paper towels. Set aside.

4. In a medium bowl, use a wire whisk to combine eggs, milk and the 1 teaspoon vegetable oil. Fold in flour, ¼ cup at time, stirring each time to distribute ingredients. (Batter should be thick enough to scoop with a spoon and hold its shape.) Stir asparagus into batter.

5. In a large saucepan or deep-fat fryer, heat 3 to 4 inches oil over medium-high to 325°. Use rounded measuring tablespoon or small ice cream scoop to drop asparagus mixture into hot oil, being careful of splattering oil.

6. Fry, a few fritters at a time, for 3 to 5 minutes or until golden, turning several times with a slotted metal spoon. Maintain oil temperature at about 325°. If browning too quickly, lower the heat to medium. Remove fritters from the hot oil using the slotted spoon. Drain on wire racks set over paper towels. Serve immediately with Lemon Garlic Aioli. **Makes 8 to 10 servings.**

Lemon Garlic Aioli: In a medium bowl, stir together ½ cup mayonnaise and 3 tablespoons milk. Stir in ½ teaspoon lemon zest, 2 teaspoons lemon juice and 2 cloves garlic, minced.

*Note: As a substitute for the self-rising flour, use 2½ cups all-purpose flour plus 2½ teaspoons baking powder, 1½ teaspoons salt and ¾ teaspoon baking soda.

Per serving: 406 cal, 27 g fat, 78 mg chol, 1,348 mg sodium, 32 g carbo, 2 g fiber, 8 g pro.

Arugula Pesto

Pesto is usually based on basil. This version features the nutty, peppery taste of arugula instead.

PREP 15 minutes **COOK** 5 minutes

½ cup walnuts
¼ cup finely shredded Parmesan cheese
    (1 ounce)
 4 cloves garlic, halved
 2 cups firmly packed fresh baby arugula,
    fresh baby spinach or fresh basil leaves
½ cup olive oil
    Salt

1. In a heavy medium skillet, toast walnuts over medium heat for 5 to 7 minutes or until you smell the walnuts, shaking skillet once or twice during toasting. Remove the skillet from heat and let the walnuts cool a few minutes.

2. In a food processor or blender, combine walnuts, Parmesan and garlic. Cover and process or blend with several on/off turns until walnuts are coarsely chopped. Add arugula. Cover and process or blend with several on/off turns until leaves are coarsely chopped.

3. With the machine running, gradually add olive oil and process or blend to the consistency of soft butter. If you prefer a smooth, thin pesto, add more oil. If you want a thicker, chunkier pesto, add a little less. Season to taste with salt.

4. If you're not serving the pesto immediately, divide into three ⅓-cup portions. Place portions in small airtight containers and store in the refrigerator up to 2 days or freeze for up to 3 months.

5. Use as a spread for lightly toasted sourdough or French bread. Or toss the pesto with hot, cooked pasta (one portion of the pesto is enough for 12 ounces pasta). **Makes 1 cup pesto.**

Per 2 tablespoons: 181 cal, 19 g fat, 2 mg chol, 117 mg sodium, 2 g carbo, 1 g fiber, 2 g pro.

Flowers—whether artfully arranged in a flower box or emerging from the forest floor—signal the arrival of spring. Trillium (far right) is one of the most common woodland wildflowers in the Midwest.

Spring Greens Soup

PREP 20 minutes **COOK** 15 minutes

    1 medium onion, halved and sliced
    1 tablespoon cooking oil
    3 cups reduced-sodium chicken broth or
        vegetable broth
    ¼ to ½ teaspoon freshly ground black
        pepper
   12 ounces Yukon gold potatoes, quartered
    3 cups sliced fresh mushrooms (optional)
    2 tablespoons butter (optional)
    3 cups fresh spinach leaves
    3 cups fresh arugula leaves
    2 cups fresh Italian (flat-leaf) parsley leaves
        and tender stems
      Salt
      Fresh arugula

1. In a 3-quart saucepan, cook onion in hot oil over medium heat for 5 minutes. Add broth and pepper. Bring to boiling. Add potatoes and return to boiling; reduce heat. Simmer, covered, 10 minutes.

2. Meanwhile, in a large skillet, cook mushrooms, if using, in butter over medium heat 6 to 8 minutes until tender and liquid has evaporated; set aside.

3. Remove saucepan from heat. Use immersion blender to blend onion-potato mixture until almost smooth. Add spinach, arugula and parsley. Return to heat. Bring to boiling; remove from heat. Using immersion blender, blend soup again until nearly smooth and flecks of green remain. Season to taste with salt. Serve immediately, topped with sautéed mushrooms, if you like, and additional fresh arugula. **Makes 6 appetizer or side-dish servings.**

Per serving: 92 cal, 3 g fat, 0 mg chol, 412 mg sodium, 14 g carbo, 3 g fiber, 4 g pro.

Pea-Shoot Soup

This fresh-tasting soup uses pea shoots—the tiny, tender leaves and vines of young pea plants—found at farmers markets in late spring. Can't find them? Substitute baby spinach.

START TO FINISH 30 minutes

    1 14.5-ounce can vegetable broth or stock
    ¼ cup whipping cream
    2 cups firmly packed pea shoots, ends
        trimmed (about 4 ounces)
    1 cup finely chopped spring onions or
        green onions
    2 tablespoons olive oil
    ¼ teaspoon salt
    ¼ teaspoon freshly ground black pepper
    2 tablespoons butter, softened

1. In a large saucepan, bring stock and cream to boiling; reduce heat. Simmer, uncovered, for 5 minutes.

2. In a large skillet, cook and stir pea shoots and spring onions in hot oil over medium-high heat for 1 to 2 minutes or until pea shoots wilt and onions are tender. Add salt and pepper.

3. Add pea-shoot mixture to stock mixture. Simmer, uncovered, 2 to 3 minutes or until heated through. Using immersion blender, blend until vegetable mixture is almost smooth. (Or transfer mixture to a food processor or blender.* Cover and process or blend until mixture is almost smooth.) Stir butter into vegetable puree. Season to taste. Serve immediately. **Makes 4 appetizer or side-dish servings.**

*Note: If using a blender, remove center cap in lid; cover lid with clean kitchen towel to prevent splattering and let steam from hot liquid safely escape.

Per serving: 192 cal, 18 g fat, 36 mg chol, 617 mg sodium, 7 g carbo, 2 g fiber, 2 g pro.

Spring is the season of "green up"—both outside and on the table. After months of brown earth, hearty stews and root vegetables, the fresh green foods refresh the palate and the spirit.

PEA-SHOOT SOUP

SPRING CHICKEN STEW

Spring Chicken Stew

START TO FINISH 30 minutes

 1 lemon
1¼ pounds skinless, boneless chicken thighs
    Salt and ground black pepper
 1 tablespoon olive oil
 8 ounces baby carrots with tops, scrubbed,
    trimmed and halved lengthwise
 1 12-ounce jar chicken gravy
1½ cups water
 1 tablespoon Dijon-style mustard
 2 heads baby bok choy, quartered
    Fresh lemon thyme (optional)

1. Zest lemon; set zest aside. Juice lemon and set juice aside. Season the chicken thighs lightly with salt and pepper.

2. In a Dutch oven, cook and stir chicken in hot oil over medium-high heat for 2 to 3 minutes or until chicken is browned, turning occasionally.

3. Add carrots, gravy and the water to Dutch oven. Stir in mustard. Bring to boiling. Place bok choy on top. Reduce heat. Simmer, covered, 10 minutes or just until chicken is done and vegetables are tender. Add lemon juice to taste.

4. Ladle into bowls. Top with lemon zest and, if you like, lemon thyme. **Makes 4 servings.**

Per serving: 273 cal, 12 g fat, 117 mg chol, 909 mg sodium, 13 g carbo, 3 g fiber, 31 g pro.

Sesame Pork and Noodles

Make this easy main dish ahead of time so it's chilled for a lunch or a light weekday dinner.

PREP 30 minutes   **CHILL** 2 hours

 8 ounces dried Chinese egg noodles or
    fine noodles
    Soy-Sesame Vinaigrette (recipe follows)
1½ pounds fresh asparagus spears, trimmed
    and cut into 2-inch-long pieces, or one
    16-ounce package frozen cut asparagus
 4 medium carrots, cut into thin ribbons or
    bite-size strips (2 cups)
 1 pound cooked lean pork, cut into thin
    strips
    Sesame seeds (optional)
    Sliced green onion (optional)

1. Cook noodles according to package directions; drain. Rinse with cold water until cool; drain. Meanwhile, make the Soy-Sesame Vinaigrette; chill.

2. If using fresh asparagus, cook in a covered saucepan in a small amount of lightly salted boiling water for 4 to 6 minutes or until crisp-tender. (If using frozen asparagus, cook according to package directions.) Drain well.

3. In a large bowl, combine noodles, asparagus, carrots and pork. Cover and chill in the refrigerator for 2 to 24 hours.

4. To serve, toss to coat salad with vinaigrette. If you like, add sesame seeds and green onion. **Makes 8 servings.**

Soy-Sesame Vinaigrette: In a screw-top jar, combine ½ cup reduced-sodium soy sauce, ¼ cup rice wine vinegar or vinegar, ¼ cup honey, 2 tablespoons salad oil and 2 teaspoons toasted sesame oil. Cover; shake. Chill 2 to 24 hours.

Per serving: 338 cal, 12 g fat, 71 mg chol, 654 mg sodium, 35 g carbo, 3 g fiber, 23 g pro.

Ham and Pea Soup

PREP 20 minutes   **COOK** 15 minutes

 6 ounces lower-sodium, lower-fat ham
    (1 cup), cut in bite-size pieces
 2 teaspoons canola oil
12 ounces fresh peas or one 10-ounce
    package frozen baby peas
 2 cups water
 1 14-ounce can reduced-sodium chicken
    broth
 2 medium carrots, sliced ¼ inch thick
 2 stalks celery, sliced ½ inch thick
 1 bunch green onions, bias-sliced
 1 tablespoon snipped fresh tarragon or
    ½ teaspoon dried tarragon
    Lemon wedges
½ of an 8-ounce carton nonfat yogurt

1. In a large saucepan, brown ham in hot oil over medium heat without stirring for 3 minutes. Stir and brown the other side for 2 to 3 minutes.

2. Add peas, the water, broth, carrots, celery, green onions and tarragon. Bring to boiling. Reduce heat; simmer, covered, for 5 to 10 minutes or until peas and carrots are tender.

3. To serve, divide soup among four soup bowls. Pass lemon wedges and yogurt. **Makes 4 servings.**

Per serving: 176 cal, 4 g fat, 19 mg chol, 586 mg sodium, 21 g carbo, 6 g fiber, 14 g pro.

Soba Noodle Bowl

START TO FINISH 25 minutes

- 2 14-ounce cans reduced-sodium chicken broth
- 1 cup water
- 2 6-ounce skinless, boneless chicken breast halves
- 8 ounces fresh sugar snap peas
- 2 medium carrots, thinly bias-sliced
- 6 ounces soba (buckwheat noodles)
- 1 red or green jalapeño pepper, thinly sliced and seeded*
- 2 tablespoons reduced-sodium soy sauce
  Crushed red pepper (optional)
  Snipped fresh parsley (optional)

1. In a large saucepan, bring broth and the water to boiling.

2. Meanwhile, very thinly slice the chicken; halve any large snap peas; set aside. Add chicken, carrots, soba, jalapeño and soy sauce to boiling broth mixture. Cover and cook over medium heat for 7 minutes or until chicken is cooked through and noodles are tender. Add peas and cook, covered, 3 minutes more or just until peas are tender.

3. Ladle into serving bowls. If you like, sprinkle crushed red pepper and parsley. **Makes 4 servings.**

*Note: Because chile peppers contain volatile oils that can burn your skin and eyes, avoid direct contact with them when possible. When working with chile peppers, wear plastic or rubber gloves. If your hands do touch the peppers, wash well with soap and water.

Per serving: 295 cal., 1 g fat, 49 mg chol, 1,172 mg sodium, 41 g carbo, 4 g fiber, 30 g pro.

Honey Roast Chicken with Spring Peas and Shallots

This beautiful glazed chicken is served with a light champagne-and-honey sauce. Lemon slices added during the last few minutes balance the sweetness of the honey. This easily becomes a pan stew when you use chicken pieces (see below).

PREP 15 minutes **ROAST** 1 hour 20 minutes **COOK** 13 minutes

- 1 3½- to 4-pound whole broiler-fryer chicken
- 2 tablespoons butter, melted
- ½ teaspoon each salt and black pepper
- ¾ cup honey
- 2 tablespoons fresh tarragon
- 1 cup sliced shallots
- 1 cup champagne, sparkling wine or reduced-sodium chicken broth
- ½ cup chicken broth
- 1½ cups fresh or frozen peas (optional)
- 1 small lemon, thinly sliced
  Honey (optional)

1. Rinse chicken cavity; pat chicken dry with paper towels. Skewer neck skin to back; tie legs to tail. Place in a shallow roasting pan. Brush with butter; sprinkle with salt and pepper.

2. Roast, uncovered, in a 375° oven for 1¼ to 1¾ hours or until drumsticks move easily and chicken is no longer pink (180°). Brush with half the honey and sprinkle with half the tarragon. Roast 5 minutes longer or until honey forms a golden brown glaze.

3. Remove chicken from pan and tent with foil. Transfer roasting pan to stove top. Add shallots, champagne, broth, remaining honey and fresh peas (if using). Simmer, uncovered, about 10 minutes, until juices thicken slightly and shallots are tender. Add frozen peas (if using) and lemon slices to pan. Simmer 3 to 5 minutes or until heated through. To serve, return chicken to pan, sprinkle with remaining tarragon, and, if you like, top with additional honey. **Makes 6 servings.**

Pan Stew Chicken: Use 2 bone-in chicken breast halves and 4 bone-in chicken thighs in place of the whole chicken. Arrange chicken pieces skin sides up in shallow baking pan. Brush with butter, then sprinkle with salt and pepper. Roast, uncovered, for 35 minutes. Brush with half the honey and sprinkle with half the tarragon. Roast 5 minutes longer, until honey forms a golden brown glaze. Continue as directed in Step 3.

Per serving: 811 cal, 44 g fat, 209 mg chol, 461 mg sodium, 47 g carbo, 3 g fiber, 52 g pro.

HONEY ROAST
CHICKEN WITH
SPRING PEAS AND
SHALLOTS

**HAM-AND-
ASPARAGUS-
STUFFED CHICKEN**

Ham-and-Asparagus-Stuffed Chicken

Whirl together fresh deviled ham spread in a food processor and pair with asparagus for a springy combination. The spread can be made up to two days ahead.

PREP 30 minutes **COOK** 20 minutes

    1 cup diced cooked ham, rind removed
    2 tablespoons mayonnaise
    1 tablespoon finely chopped onion
    1 tablespoon snipped fresh tarragon or
        parsley
    1 teaspoon Worcestershire sauce
    1 teaspoon cider vinegar
    1 teaspoon Dijon-style or whole-grain
        mustard
    ⅛ teaspoon cayenne pepper
      Freshly ground black pepper
    4 large skinless, boneless chicken breast
        halves (about 2 pounds)
    8 ounces green, white and/or purple
        asparagus, trimmed
      Salt and freshly ground black pepper
    1 tablespoon olive oil

1. For deviled ham: in a food processor, combine ham, mayonnaise, onion, tarragon, Worcestershire sauce, vinegar, mustard, cayenne and a few grinds of black pepper. Cover and process until ham is very finely chopped and almost smooth, scraping processor bowl as needed. Set aside deviled ham while butterflying chicken breasts or cover and refrigerate up to 2 days.

2. Butterfly chicken breasts by placing each breast half on a flat surface or cutting board. With palm on chicken and fingers away from knife blade, cut through one side of the chicken to within ¾ inch of the opposite side. Open to lie flat. Pound chicken with flat side of meat mallet to ¼-inch thickness.

3. Spread ¼ cup of the deviled ham on half of each chicken piece. Top with 3 to 5 asparagus spears. Fold remaining half over stuffing. Tie closed with 100-percent-cotton kitchen string. Sprinkle chicken with salt and pepper.

4. In a 12-inch skillet, cook chicken in hot oil over medium heat for 10 to 12 minutes per side, until browned and no longer pink (170°). **Makes 4 servings.**

Per serving: 399 cal, 17 g fat, 167 mg chol, 929 mg sodium, 3 g carbo, 1 g fiber, 54 g pro.

Herbed Cheese-Stuffed Salmon

PREP 20 minutes **BAKE** 14 minutes

    6 6-ounce fresh or frozen skinless salmon
        fillets
    1 lemon
    1 5.2-ounce container semisoft cheese with
        garlic and herbs
      Sea salt or salt
    1 cup soft bread crumbs (about 1½ slices)
    ⅓ cup freshly shredded Parmesan cheese
        (1½ ounces)
    ¼ cup butter, melted
    2 tablespoons pine nuts, toasted

1. Thaw fish, if frozen. Rinse fish; pat dry. Zest lemon to make 2 teaspoons; cut lemon in wedges and set aside. In a small bowl, combine semisoft cheese and lemon zest. In top of each fillet, from about ½ inch from one edge, cut a pocket, taking care not to cut all the way through the fish. (If fillet is thin, cut into the fish at an angle.) Spoon cheese mixture into pockets. Season fish with salt. Place in shallow baking pan. Set aside.

2. In a small bowl, combine bread crumbs, Parmesan cheese, butter and pine nuts; sprinkle over fillets, pressing lightly. Bake, uncovered, in 425° oven about 14 minutes or until salmon flakes when tested with a fork. Serve with lemon wedges. **Makes 6 servings.**

Per serving: 537 cal, 40 g fat, 125 mg chol, 561 mg sodium, 7 g carbo, 1 g fiber, 38 g pro.

Asparagus brings a fresh taste to every meal. Its delicate flavor works as well with a rich creamy sauce as it does tossed in a light citrusy dressing.

MOREL AND
ASPARAGUS
CRISPY PIZZA

Morel and Asparagus Crispy Pizza

PREP 30 minutes **RISE** 1 hour **BAKE** 12 minutes per batch

    1 package active dry yeast
 1¼ cups warm water (105° to 115°)
    2 to 2¼ cups all-purpose flour
 1½ cups semolina flour
    3 tablespoons olive oil
    2 teaspoons salt
    2 teaspoons sugar
 10 ounces morel mushrooms, cleaned and
         sliced ½ inch thick
    1 tablespoon butter
  ½ cup sliced shallots (about 4)
  ¼ cup dry white wine
    2 teaspoons snipped fresh thyme
    8 ounces thin asparagus, cleaned, trimmed
         and cut into 2-inch pieces
         Cornmeal
         Olive oil
    8 ounces Gruyère cheese, shredded (2 cups)
         Cracked black pepper

1. In a large bowl, combine yeast and the water. Let stand until yeast is dissolved; about 5 minutes.

2. Add 2 cups all-purpose flour, the semolina flour, 3 tablespoons olive oil, the salt and sugar. Mix by hand or on low speed of an electric mixer until well combined. Turn out onto a lightly floured surface. Knead in enough of the remaining all-purpose flour to form a smooth elastic dough, 6 to 8 minutes.

3. Transfer dough to a bowl lightly coated with additional olive oil, turning to coat sides. Cover and let rise in a warm place until about doubled in size, 1 to 1½ hours.

4. Meanwhile, in a large skillet, cook and stir mushrooms in hot butter over medium-high heat for 2 to 3 minutes or until mushrooms just begin to soften. Add shallots, wine and thyme. Cook and stir for 4 to 6 minutes or until shallots are tender. Add asparagus; cook and stir for 2 minutes. Remove from heat.

5. Grease and dust two extra-large baking sheets with cornmeal. Punch dough down and divide dough in half. On a lightly floured surface, roll out one portion of the dough to ⅛ inch thickness (don't worry if it's not perfectly round). Transfer to a prepared baking sheet.

6. Brush lightly with additional olive oil. Top with half the mushroom mixture and half the cheese; season with pepper. Bake in 475° oven on lowest rack 12 minutes or until crispy and brown. While first pizza bakes, repeat with remaining dough and toppings. **Makes 8 servings.**

Per serving: 458 cal, 18 g fat, 35 mg chol, 694 mg sodium, 54 g carbo, 3 g fiber, 18 g pro.

Spring Pasta with Morels, Ramps and Peas

(Pictured on page 6.)

START TO FINISH 35 minutes

 12 ounces fresh morel mushrooms, cleaned
         and very coarsely chopped
    4 to 6 ounces ramps, cleaned and cut into
         ½-inch pieces; or 1 medium leek, cleaned
         and thinly sliced, plus 1 clove garlic, minced
    1 tablespoon butter
  ¼ cup diced cooked ham
  ¼ cup dry white wine
  ¾ cup whipping cream
  ½ cup reduced-sodium chicken broth
 1¼ cups frozen peas, thawed
 1½ teaspoons snipped fresh thyme
         Salt and cracked black pepper
 10 ounces dried linguine pasta
  ¼ cup chopped fresh Italian (flat-leaf)
         parsley or regular parsley
         Shaved Parmesan cheese (optional)

1. In a very large skillet, cook and stir morels and ramps in hot butter over medium-high heat for 4 to 5 minutes or until just tender. Using a slotted spoon, transfer mixture to a bowl.

2. Add ham to skillet. Cook and stir for 3 to 4 minutes, until ham starts to brown. Remove skillet from heat. Add wine. Return skillet to heat and cook for 1 minute. Add whipping cream and broth. Cook, stirring occasionally, for 6 to 8 minutes or until sauce coats the back of a wooden spoon. Return morels to skillet with peas and thyme. Cook for 3 to 4 minutes or until peas are just tender. Season to taste.

3. Cook linguine according to package directions; drain. Add sauce and parsley to linguine in pot over low heat. Toss mixture until well combined. Serve with Parmesan, if you like. **Makes 4 servings.**

Per serving: 541 cal, 22 g fat, 74 mg chol, 429 mg sodium, 68 g carbo, 6 g fiber, 17 g pro.

At Midwest wildlife preserves, spring arrives on the wings of migrant birds. At the 33,000-acre Horicon Marsh in southern Wisconsin, visitors have spotted nearly 300 species of birds, including varieties of heron, kingfishers, cormorants, swans, woodpeckers, wrens, falcons, cranes and swallows.

Napa Cabbage and Black Bean Slaw

PREP 25 minutes **COOK** 15 minutes
STAND 5 minutes

 1 12-ounce bottle chili sauce
 ¼ cup packed brown sugar
 1 tablespoon lime juice
 1 teaspoon red wine vinegar
 ½ cup olive oil
 3 cups shredded Napa cabbage
 1 cup jicama cut into matchstick-size pieces
 ½ of a 15-ounce can black beans, rinsed
    and drained
 ¼ cup thinly sliced red onion cut into
    quarters
    Dash salt
    Dash freshly ground black pepper

1. For dressing: In a medium saucepan, combine chili sauce and brown sugar. Bring to boiling; reduce heat. Simmer, uncovered, about 15 minutes or until mixture is reduced to about 1 cup. Remove from heat; let cool slightly. Whisk in lime juice and vinegar. Slowly add oil in a thin, steady stream (dressing will thicken as oil is added), whisking constantly.

2. In a large salad bowl, combine cabbage, jicama, black beans and red onion. Sprinkle with salt and pepper. Drizzle about half of the dressing over cabbage mixture; toss to coat. Season to taste. Let stand 5 minutes before serving.

3. Cover and refrigerate remaining dressing for up to 1 week. Use as a dressing or dipping sauce. **Makes 6 servings.**

Per serving: 290 cal, 18 g fat, 0 mg chol, 924 mg sodium, 29 g carbo, 7 g fiber, 3 g pro.

Crisp Portobello Mushroom and Spring Carrot Salad

Carrots are in season in both spring and fall, but spring carrots are the sweetest.

PREP 30 minutes **COOK** 11 minutes

 16 young, small spring carrots with tops
    Salt and black pepper
 3 tablespoons sherry wine vinegar or white
    wine vinegar
 1 tablespoon honey
 1 to 2 teaspoons Dijon-style mustard
 3 tablespoons olive oil
 4 3- to 4-ounce portobello mushrooms
 ½ cup all-purpose flour
 2 eggs, lightly beaten
 1 cup panko (Japanese-style bread crumbs)
 ½ cup olive oil
 2 ounces semisoft goat cheese (chèvre),
    crumbled
 1 teaspoon snipped fresh chives

1. Peel carrots; remove tops and trim. Scrub carrots with vegetable brush; rinse. In a covered medium saucepan, cook carrots in small amount of boiling, lightly salted water for 7 to 9 minutes or until tender; drain and cool slightly. Cut carrots in half lengthwise. Transfer to a large bowl and sprinkle with some salt and pepper.

2. In a small bowl, whisk together vinegar, honey and mustard. Slowly add the 3 tablespoons oil in thin, steady stream while whisking (vinaigrette will thicken). Drizzle the vinaigrette over the carrots; toss to coat. Set carrots aside.

3. Cut off mushroom stems even with surface of caps; discard stems. Using a spoon, remove gills under caps. Lightly rinse caps; wipe with clean, damp cloth or paper towel. Gently pat dry with paper towels. Sprinkle both sides of mushrooms with salt and pepper.

4. Place flour in shallow dish. Place eggs in a second dish. Place panko in a third dish. Coat mushrooms with flour; dip in eggs, then dip in panko to coat all sides.

5. In a large skillet, heat the ½ cup olive oil over medium heat. Carefully add mushrooms to the hot oil. Cook for 4 to 8 minutes or until the mushrooms are golden and cooked through, turning once halfway through cooking time. Transfer to a cutting board and cut the warm mushrooms in half.

6. Place 2 mushroom halves on each salad plate. Remove carrots from vinaigrette; arrange in the center of mushrooms. Sprinkle with cheese and chives.
Makes 4 servings.

Per serving: 608 cal, 45 g fat, 104 mg chol, 421 mg sodium, 41 g carbo, 5 g fiber, 12 g pro.

CRISP PORTOBELLO
MUSHROOM AND SPRING
CARROT SALAD

**SWEET CURRY
CARROTS WITH
CHIVE YOGURT**

Sweet Curry Carrots with Chive Yogurt

Roasting brings out carrots' natural sweetness, which honey and curry enhances.

PREP 20 minutes **ROAST** 25 minutes

1½ pounds carrots with tops, trimmed (about 10)
 1 tablespoon extra-virgin olive oil
 ¼ teaspoon salt
 3 tablespoons honey
 1 tablespoon curry powder
 ⅔ cup plain low-fat Greek yogurt
 ¼ cup snipped fresh chives
 ¼ teaspoon salt

1. Scrub carrots and peel, if desired. Halve any large carrots lengthwise.

2. Line a 15x10x1-inch baking pan with foil. Toss carrots with olive oil. Evenly spread carrots in prepared pan. Sprinkle with ¼ teaspoon salt. Roast carrots in a 425° oven for 15 minutes. Meanwhile, in a small microwave-safe bowl, warm honey in microwave for 30 seconds. Whisk in curry powder; set aside.

3. Remove carrots from oven. Drizzle with honey mixture; toss to coat. Roast 10 minutes longer, turning occasionally, until carrots are glazed and tender when pierced with a fork. Transfer to platter.

4. For Chive Yogurt: In a bowl, combine yogurt, chives and ¼ teaspoon salt. Serve with carrots. **Makes 6 to 8 servings.**

Per serving: 121 cal, 3 g fat, 1 mg chol, 283 mg sodium, 21 g carb, 4 g fiber, 4 g pro.

Red Potato Salad with Mustard Dressing

This recipe has a range of vegetables to choose from, so you can build the salad to your liking.

PREP 45 minutes **ROAST** 30 minutes **CHILL** 6 hours

 3 pounds small round red potatoes, scrubbed and cut in thin wedges
 2 tablespoons olive oil
 Salt and black pepper
 Mustard Dressing (recipe follows)
 Watercress, spinach or salad greens
 ½ of a red onion, cut in thin wedges
 3 to 4 cups sliced vegetables, such as carrots, fennel and/or celery
 1 to 2 pints yellow or red cherry tomatoes, whole or halved

1. Toss potatoes with oil. Divide evenly among two well-greased 15x10x1-inch baking pans or shallow roasting pans. Sprinkle with salt and pepper. Roast, uncovered, in a 450° oven about 30 minutes, or until tender and browned, turning once with a metal spatula. Cool slightly; transfer to large bowl.

2. Meanwhile, prepare Mustard Dressing. Gently toss potatoes with about ¼ cup of the dressing. Transfer remaining dressing to a small jar or pitcher for serving. Cover and refrigerate potatoes and remaining dressing for 6 to 24 hours. Let potatoes stand at room temperature for 30 minutes before serving. To serve, arrange potatoes with remaining ingredients as directed in Plated, Layered and Chopped salads. **Makes 12 servings.**

Mustard Dressing: In a blender, combine ⅔ cup white wine vinegar, ⅔ cup olive oil, ½ cup light or regular mayonnaise, ¼ cup hot mustard or stone-ground mustard, ½ teaspoon salt and ¼ teaspoon black pepper. Process until blended.

Plated:

1. Prepare Red Potato Salad.

2. Arrange potatoes, watercress, onion, vegetables and tomatoes on plates. Pass Mustard Dressing. **Makes 12 servings.**

Per serving: 280 cal, 18 g fat, 4 mg chol, 426 mg sodium, 26 g carbo, 4 g fiber, 4 g pro.

Layered:

1. Prepare Red Potato Salad, except after removing ¼ cup of the dressing for tossing with potatoes, add an additional cup of mayonnaise to blender; blend until smooth. Transfer to a bowl; cover and refrigerate.

2. Layer spinach in bottom of a large straight-sided clear glass cylinder or jar (about 1½ gallons). Layer potatoes, onion, 2 cups of vegetables, 1 to 2 pints cherry tomatoes and remaining 1 to 2 cups vegetables. Spoon on half the dressing. Serve at once or cover and refrigerate overnight. Pass remaining dressing. **Makes 12 servings.**

Per serving: 354 cal, 25 g fat, 11 mg chol, 569 mg sodium, 30 g carbo, 5 g fiber, 4 g pro.

Chopped:

1. Prepare Red Potato Salad. Coarsely chop roasted potatoes, onion and sliced vegetables. Toss with greens, tomatoes and some of the dressing.

2. Serve in individual cups with remaining dressing on the side. **Makes 12 servings.**

Just-Right Rhubarb Pie

This sweet-tart pie was inspired by food vendors at RAGBRAI, the Register's Annual Great Bike Ride Across Iowa.

PREP 25 minutes   **STAND** 15 minutes   **BAKE** 50 minutes

1 cup sugar
3 tablespoons quick-cooking tapioca
2 teaspoons orange zest
½ teaspoon ground cinnamon or
   ¼ teaspoon ground nutmeg (optional)
5 cups fresh or frozen (thawed and drained)
   sliced rhubarb
   Flaky Pie Pastry (recipe follows) or one
   15-ounce package (2 crusts) rolled
   refrigerated unbaked piecrust
2 tablespoons butter, cut up
1 egg, lightly beaten
1 tablespoon water
   Sugar
   Vanilla ice cream (optional)

1. In a large bowl, combine 1 cup sugar, the tapioca, orange zest and, if you like, cinnamon. Add rhubarb. Gently toss to coat. Cover; let stand for 15 minutes, stirring once.

2. Meanwhile, prepare Flaky Pie Pastry. On a lightly floured surface, slightly flatten one portion of dough. Roll dough into a 12-inch circle. Wrap pastry circle around rolling pin; unroll into a 9-inch pie plate. Ease pastry into pie plate without stretching. Trim pastry even with edge of pie plate.

3. Spoon rhubarb mixture into pastry-lined pie plate. Dot with butter.

4. Roll the remaining dough into a 12-inch circle. Cut slits in pastry to allow steam to escape. Place pastry circle on filling; trim pastry to ½ inch beyond edge of pie plate. Fold top pastry edge under bottom pastry. Crimp edge as desired.

5. In a small bowl, combine beaten egg and the water; brush lightly over pastry. Sprinkle with additional sugar.

6. To prevent overbrowning, cover edge of pie with foil. Place a foil-lined baking sheet on oven rack below pie.

7. Bake pie in a 400° oven for 25 minutes. Remove foil. Bake for 25 minutes more or until top is golden and center of filling is bubbly. Serve warm with ice cream, if you like, or cool completely on wire rack. **Makes 8 servings.**

Flaky Pie Pastry: In a large bowl, combine 2½ cups all-purpose flour and 1 teaspoon salt. Using pastry blender, cut in ½ cup cold shortening and ¼ cup cold butter until pieces are pea size. Sprinkle 1 tablespoon ice water over part of the mixture; gently toss with a fork. Push moistened dough to side of bowl. Repeat using 1 tablespoon of ice water at a time, until all the dough is moistened (½ to ⅔ cup total). Knead gently until dough holds together. Divide pastry in half; form halves into balls. Continue as directed.

Per serving: 470 cal, 22 g fat, 46 mg chol, 380 mg sodium, 63 g carbo, 3 g fiber, 6 g pro.

Ample amounts of sugar tame the tart flavor of rhubarb in homey pies, crisps, cobblers and crumbles. Desserts made with this humble vegetable are a late-spring treat throughout the Midwest.

Blueberry-Rhubarb Cobbler

PREP 30 minutes **BAKE** 25 minutes

1½ cups sliced fresh or frozen rhubarb,
    thawed
¼ cup sugar
¼ cup orange marmalade
2 teaspoons orange zest (set aside)
3 tablespoons orange juice
1½ tablespoons quick-cooking tapioca
6 tablespoons butter
¼ teaspoon ground cinnamon
¼ teaspoon ground ginger
⅛ teaspoon ground cardamom
⅛ teaspoon ground nutmeg
3½ cups fresh or frozen blueberries
1 cup all-purpose flour
⅓ cup almond flour
⅓ cup sugar
2 teaspoons baking powder
½ teaspoon salt
½ cup whipping cream
¾ teaspoon almond extract
3 tablespoons sliced almonds
2 tablespoons turbinado (raw) sugar
    Vanilla ice cream (optional)

1. Dice rhubarb. In a large nonstick oven-going skillet, combine rhubarb, ¼ cup sugar, marmalade, orange juice, tapioca and 1 tablespoon of the butter. Cook and stir until bubbly. Stir in cinnamon, ginger, cardamom, nutmeg and blueberries; cook and stir just to boiling. Remove from heat.

2. In a large bowl, whisk flours, ⅓ cup sugar, baking powder, orange zest and salt. Using a pastry blender, cut in remaining butter until pea-size. In a bowl, mix cream and extract; stir into flour mixture. Drop dough in 8 mounds over filling; sprinkle with almonds and sugar.

3. Bake in 375° oven 25 to 28 minutes or until a pick inserted into biscuit comes out clean. Cool on wire rack. Serve warm or at room temperature. If you like, serve with ice cream. **Makes 8 servings.**

Per serving: 372 cal, 18 g fat, 43 mg chol, 326 mg sodium, 51 g carbo, 3 g fiber, 4 g pro.

Flowering trees line the walking paths in Cincinnati's Eden Park, located on a hill northeast of downtown. The paths offer views of the Ohio River and historical Krohn Conservatory.

Meringue with Seared Pineapple

PREP 30 minutes **BAKE** 35 minutes **STAND** 1 hour

    5 eggs
    2 teaspoons vanilla
    ¼ teaspoon cream of tartar
    ¾ cups granulated sugar
      Pineapple-Lime Curd (recipe follows)
    ½ of a pineapple, peeled, cored and sliced
    2 tablespoons butter
    2 tablespoons packed brown sugar
      Sliced Key limes (optional)
      Fresh mint (optional)

1. Separate egg yolks and whites. Set yolks aside for Pineapple-Lime Curd. For meringue, let whites stand at room temperature for 30 minutes. Line a baking sheet with parchment paper. In a large mixing bowl, beat egg whites, vanilla and cream of tartar with an electric mixer on medium-high speed until soft peaks form. Beating on high, add granulated sugar, 1 tablespoon at a time, until stiff peaks form (about 8 minutes total).

2. Spread meringue on prepared baking sheet to make large oval (about 13x9 inches), building up edges slightly to form a nest. Bake in a 300° oven for 35 minutes. Turn off oven; let stand 1 hour. Carefully lift meringue off paper and transfer to serving platter. Meanwhile, prepare Pineapple-Lime Curd.

3. In a 12-inch skillet, cook pineapple slices in hot butter for 8 minutes or until browned, turning once. Sprinkle slices with brown sugar. Cook pineapple, uncovered, for 1 to 2 minutes more or until sugar is dissolved.

4. To assemble, fill meringue nest with Pineapple-Lime Curd and top with seared pineapple slices. Drizzle with juice from seared pineapple. Serve at once topped with Key limes and mint, if you like.
Makes 10 servings.

Per serving: 297 cal, 14 g fat, 136 mg chol, 118 mg sodium, 41 g carbo, 0 g fiber, 4 g pro.

Pineapple-Lime Curd: In a medium saucepan, combine ¾ cup granulated sugar and 1 tablespoon cornstarch. Stir in ¼ cup lime juice, ⅓ cup water and ¼ cup pineapple juice concentrate. Cook and stir over medium heat until thickened and bubbly. In a medium bowl, whisk together 5 reserved egg yolks until smooth. Gradually whisk half of the hot juice mixture into the yolks. Return yolk-juice mixture to saucepan. Cook and stir until mixture thickens and comes to a gentle boil. Cook and stir 2 minutes more. Remove from heat; stir in ½ cup butter, cut up, until melted. Transfer to bowl. Cover and refrigerate.

With fabulously fresh ingredients and sandwiches named the likes of "Mr. Wubbly's Fat Bass" and "Hazardous Waist," the Lake Street Market in SoBo—an artsy district of Boyne City, Michigan—has cultivated a devoted following.

Pineapple Upside-Down Cake

PREP 25 minutes **BAKE** 35 minutes **COOL** 25 minutes

½ cup butter
1 cup packed brown sugar
12 canned pineapple rings in juice*
2 cups all-purpose flour
2 teaspoons baking powder
½ teaspoon salt
¼ teaspoon ground nutmeg
½ cup butter, softened
½ cup granulated sugar
½ cup packed brown sugar
2 eggs
½ cup milk
1 teaspoon vanilla
1 cup vanilla Greek yogurt or sweetened
    whipped cream (optional)
1 tablespoon packed brown sugar (optional)
12 maraschino cherries (optional)

1. Grease the bottom and sides of a 13x9x2-inch baking pan. Line bottom of pan with parchment paper; set pan aside.

2. For topping: In a medium saucepan, melt ½ cup butter over low heat. Stir in the 1 cup brown sugar. Bring mixture to boiling over medium heat, stirring frequently. Pour into prepared pan. Drain pineapple rings, reserving ½ cup juice. Fit rings tightly into bottom of pan. Save any extra rings for another use.

3. For cake: In a medium bowl, whisk together flour, baking powder, salt and nutmeg; set aside. In a large mixing bowl, beat ½ cup softened butter, the granulated sugar and the ½ cup brown sugar with an electric mixer on medium speed for 2 minutes, scraping sides of bowl occasionally. Beat in eggs until combined. Beat in half of the flour mixture on low speed. Beat in the reserved pineapple juice, the milk and vanilla until combined. Beat in the remaining flour mixture. Spread batter carefully over pineapple slices in pan.

4. Bake in a 350° oven for 35 to 40 minutes or until a toothpick inserted in center comes out clean. Cool in pan on a wire rack for 10 minutes. Loosen sides of cake; invert onto a serving plate. If any pineapple sticks to pan, gently replace on cake. Let cool at least 15 minutes; serve warm or cooled. If you like, in a small bowl, combine yogurt and the 1 tablespoon brown sugar. Rinse cherries; pat dry with paper towels. Serve cake topped with yogurt mixture and cherries. **Makes 12 servings.**

*Tip: You will need one 20-ounce can and one 8-ounce can pineapple slices for the 12 slices. There will be a few slices of leftover pineapple.

To store: Loosely cover cake or mini cakes. Store at room temperature for up to 24 hours.

Per serving: 396 cal, 17 g fat, 77 mg chol, 290 mg sodium, 60 g carbo, 1 g fiber, 4 g pro.

This classic from the 1950s and '60s is experiencing a renaissance. Serve it at the next gathering at your house or bring it to a potluck and enjoy the enthusiasm it inspires.

Lemon-Rosemary Cheesecake

PREP 30 minutes **BAKE** 40 minutes
STAND 1 hour 45 minutes **CHILL** 4 hours

- 2 15-ounce cartons ricotta cheese
- ⅓ cup butter
- ½ cup granulated sugar
- ⅓ cup all-purpose flour
- 1 tablespoon baking powder
- 1 teaspoon vanilla
- 3 slightly beaten eggs
- 1 tablespoon snipped fresh rosemary
- 2 teaspoons lemon zest
- ¼ cup chopped pistachio nuts

1. Let cheese and butter stand at room temperature for 30 minutes to soften. Grease and lightly flour a 9-inch springform pan.

2. In a large mixing bowl, beat butter and sugar until light and fluffy. Beat in ricotta, flour, baking powder and vanilla until combined. Stir in eggs, rosemary and lemon zest just until combined. Pour into prepared pan.

3. Bake in a 300° oven for 40 minutes. Turn off oven; let cheesecake remain in oven for 1 hour. Remove; cool cheesecake in pan on wire rack for 15 minutes. Using a small sharp knife, loosen cheesecake from sides of pan; cool for 30 minutes. Remove sides of pan; cool cheesecake completely on rack. Cover and refrigerate at least 4 hours. Top with pistachios. **Makes 12 servings.**

Per serving: 245 cal, 17 g fat, 102 mg chol, 184 mg sodium, 14 g carb, 11 g pro.

Irresistible Tiramisu

Be sure to use either crisp ladyfingers or dry the soft ones so that the cookies just get pleasantly soft—not mushy—when brushed with the coffee mixture.

PREP 45 minutes **CHILL** 4 to 24 hours

- ¾ cup freshly brewed hot espresso or very strong coffee
- ¾ cup granulated sugar
- 2 tablespoons coffee liqueur, amaretto or hazelnut liqueur (optional)
- 2 8-ounce cartons mascarpone cheese or two 8-ounce packages cream cheese, softened
- ¾ cup powdered sugar
- 1 teaspoon vanilla
- 1 cup whipping cream
- ¼ cup powdered sugar
- 1 teaspoon vanilla
- 48 savoiardi (crisp Italian ladyfingers) or two 3-ounce packages soft unfilled ladyfingers (24 total), split and dried
- 2 tablespoons unsweetened cocoa powder or finely grated semisweet chocolate

1. For syrup: In a small bowl, combine hot espresso, sugar and, if you like, coffee liqueur, stirring until sugar dissolves. Let cool to room temperature. (Or in a small saucepan, combine ¾ cup granulated sugar, ¾ cup water and 3 to 4 teaspoons instant espresso powder or instant coffee crystals. Bring to boiling over medium heat, stirring until sugar dissolves. Boil 1 minute; remove from heat. If you like, stir in coffee liqueur; continue as directed.)

2. For filling: In a medium bowl, mix mascarpone, the ¾ cup powdered sugar and 1 teaspoon vanilla. In a chilled large mixing bowl, beat whipping cream and ¼ cup powdered sugar with electric mixer until soft peaks form. Using spatula, gently fold whipped cream into mascarpone mixture.

3. Arrange one-third of the ladyfingers in bottom of 11x7x1½-inch baking dish (2-quart rectangular), trimming to fit as needed. Brush ladyfingers with one-third of the coffee syrup or quickly dip ladyfingers, one at a time, into the syrup. Spread one-third of the filling evenly over ladyfingers. Sift 2 teaspoons cocoa powder over top. Repeat layering with another one-third of the ladyfingers, one-third of the syrup and one-third of the filling. Sift 2 teaspoons of the cocoa powder over top. Top with the remaining ladyfingers; brush with the remaining syrup. Spread the remaining filling evenly over top.

4. Cover; chill 4 to 24 hours. Sift the remaining 2 teaspoons of the cocoa powder over top to serve. **Makes 16 servings.**

Per serving: 335 cal, 19 g fat, 75 mg chol, 41 mg sodium, 40 g carbo, 1 g fiber, 8 g pro.

IRRESISTIBLE
TIRAMISU

Cream-Filled Cannoli

If you don't have the time or inclination to make cannoli shells, look for premade shells at an Italian market.

PREP 45 minutes   **COOK** 2 minutes per batch   **CHILL** 2 hours

Homemade Cannoli Shells (recipe follows)
   or two 3-ounce packages cannoli shells
   (12 shells total)
2 15-ounce containers ricotta cheese
¾ cup powdered sugar
2 to 3 teaspoons vanilla
2 to 3 teaspoons dark rum (optional)
½ cup miniature semisweet chocolate pieces
1 egg white, lightly beaten
   Vegetable oil for deep-fat frying
   Powdered sugar (optional)
   Miniature semisweet chocolate pieces
   (optional)

1. If using Homemade Cannoli Shells, prepare dough. If ricotta cheese is liquidy, place in sieve or colander lined with two layers of 100-percent-cotton cheesecloth set over a bowl; strain the mixture for at least 1 hour. Discard the liquid.

2. For filling: In a bowl, mix ricotta, the ¾ cup powdered sugar, vanilla and, if you like, rum until almost smooth. Stir in chocolate pieces. Cover; chill at least 2 hours.

3. On a lightly floured surface, roll each dough portion to slightly less than ⅛ inch thickness. Make a 6x4-inch oval out of paper and use it as a pattern to cut ovals from the dough. (Do not reroll trimmings.) Beginning with long side, roll each oval loosely around one end of greased metal cannoli cylinders. Moisten overlapping dough with egg white; press gently to seal.

4. In a 3-quart saucepan or deep-fat fryer, heat 3 inches vegetable oil to 375°. Fry cannoli shells, a few at a time, 1 to 2 minutes or until golden. Using tongs, gently lift shells from hot oil; drain oil from metal cylinders back into pan. Drain on paper towels; cool. When cool enough to handle, remove metal cylinders from shells. Cool cylinders before reusing. (You will need three or four cannoli cylinders.) Cool completely.

5. To serve, spoon filling into decorating bag fitted with ½-inch round tip (or spoon into resealable plastic bag; seal and snip off small corner). Pipe into homemade or purchased shells. Arrange on serving platter. If you like, sprinkle additional powdered sugar over shells and chocolate pieces over filling. Serve immediately.
Makes 12 servings.

Homemade Cannoli Shells: In a bowl, mix 2 cups all-purpose flour, 2 tablespoons sugar, 1 teaspoon unsweetened cocoa powder, ¼ teaspoon salt, ¼ teaspoon ground cinnamon and ⅛ teaspoon baking soda. Using a pastry blender, cut 2 tablespoons cold butter and 2 tablespoons shortening into flour mixture until mixture resembles coarse crumbs. In a small bowl, combine 2 well-beaten eggs and ¼ cup sweet Marsala wine (or 3 tablespoons cold water and 1 tablespoon red wine vinegar). Add egg mixture to flour mixture; stir until mixture forms a ball. Turn out onto lightly floured surface. Knead until smooth and elastic (5 to 7 minutes). Divide in half; slightly flatten. Cover; chill 1 hour.

Per cannoli: 441 cal, 27 g fat, 76 mg chol, 183 mg sodium, 38 g carbo, 1 g fiber, 12 g pro.

ROASTED PEACH PIES WITH
BUTTERSCOTCH SAUCE,
PAGE 111

Summer

Strawberry and Mango Smoothies

Vendors serving the thousands of bicyclists riding across the state of Iowa on an annual bike ride sell smoothies very similar to this refreshing, rejuvenating blend.

START TO FINISH 10 minutes

1 cup unsweetened pineapple juice or orange juice
1 small ripe banana, sliced
2 tablespoons honey (optional)
1 cup fresh strawberries, halved, or frozen unsweetened whole strawberries
1 small fresh mango, seeded, peeled and cut up (about ¾ cup)
1 cup ice cubes or crushed ice
Fresh whole strawberries and/or mango chunks (optional)

1. In a blender, combine pineapple juice, banana and, if you like, honey; cover and blend until smooth. Add strawberries and mango; cover and blend until smooth. With blender running, add ice cubes, two at a time, through opening in the lid, blending until smooth after each addition.

2. Pour smoothie into four glasses; serve immediately. If you like, garnish servings with whole strawberries and/or mango chunks. **Makes 4 (8 ounce) servings.**

Per serving: 83 cal, 0 g fat, 0 mg chol, 3 mg sodium, 20 g carbo, 2 g fiber, 1 g pro.

Nanking Cherry Jelly

PREP 45 minutes **COOK** 26 minutes **STAND** 12 hours

3½ to 4 pounds fully ripe fresh Nanking cherries, fresh tart red cherries, or 3 16-ounce packages frozen pitted tart or sweet red cherries
1 1.75-ounce package powdered fruit pectin
4½ cups sugar

1. Wash fresh cherries under cool running tap water; drain. Stem cherries and place in an 8- to 10-quart heavy Dutch oven. Barely cover cherries with water (about 3½ cups). Bring to a simmer (boiling will reduce flavor). Simmer, uncovered, about 20 minutes or until soft and the skins start to split, mashing cherries with a potato masher during cooking. Remove from heat.

2. Ladle cherry mixture into a fine-mesh sieve over a large bowl. Press cherries through the sieve; discard pits and skins. Strain juice through the sieve or a colander lined with four layers of 100-percent-cotton cheesecloth over a large bowl. Do not squeeze cheesecloth if you want clear jelly. Measure 3½ cups liquid. Discard pulp.

3. In a 4-quart heavy Dutch oven or kettle, stir together the 3½ cups strained liquid and the pectin. Heat on high, stirring constantly, until mixture comes to a full rolling boil. Stir in sugar. Return to boiling; boil for 1 minute, stirring constantly. Remove from heat; quickly skim off foam.

4. Ladle into hot, sterilized* half-pint canning jars, leaving a ¼-inch headspace. Wipe rims; adjust lids. Process in a boiling-water canner for 5 minutes (start timing when water returns to boiling and keep the water boiling gently during processing).

5. Remove jars; cool on wire racks. When jars are completely cool, check seals. Any jars not properly sealed can be stored in the refrigerator and used within 2 to 3 days or reprocessed within 24 hours. **Makes 96 (1 tablespoon) servings.**

***Tip:** To sterilize canning jars, wash in hot, soapy water; rinse thoroughly. Immerse in boiling water for 10 minutes.

Per 1 tablespoon: 49 cal, 0 g fat, 0 mg chol, 1 mg sodium, 13 g carbo, 0 g fiber, 0 g pro.

Summer is the season of state fairs and prizewinning jams, jellies, breads, cakes, cookies and other treats. Every year, thousands of Midwest cooks submit their best recipes in hopes of a blue ribbon.

NANKING
CHERRY JELLY

Bacon-Chive
78

Bacon-Cheddar-Chive Scones

PREP 25 minutes **BAKE** 20 minutes

     2 cups all-purpose flour
     2 teaspoons baking powder
     2 teaspoons sugar
     1 teaspoon salt
   ¼ cup cold butter, cut up
     1 cup diced cheddar cheese (4 ounces)
   ¾ cup whipping cream
     6 slices bacon, crisp-cooked, drained and
          crumbled
     1 tablespoon dried chives or 2 tablespoons
          snipped fresh chives
     1 tablespoon whipping cream

1. In a large bowl, combine flour, baking powder, sugar and salt. Using a pastry blender, cut in butter until mixture resembles coarse crumbs. Stir in cheese. Make a well; set aside.

2. In a medium bowl, combine ¾ cup whipping cream, the bacon and chives. Add cream mixture all at once to flour mixture. Using a fork, stir just until moistened. (If necessary, add 1 to 2 tablespoons cream until dough holds together.)

3. On a lightly floured surface, knead dough 10 to 12 strokes or until nearly smooth. Pat into a 7-inch round. Transfer to a lightly greased large baking sheet.

4. Cut round into eight wedges. Separate wedges and lightly brush tops with 1 tablespoon whipping cream.

5. Bake in a 425° oven about 20 minutes or until golden brown. Remove scones from baking sheet; serve warm or at room temperature. **Makes 8 servings.**

Per serving: 343 cal, 22 g fat, 70 mg chol, 669 mg sodium, 26 g carbo, 1 g fiber, 10 g pro.

A warm scone and a cup of coffee enjoyed from a scenic perch on a dock enhances a quiet morning on northern Minnesota's Lake Vermillion. Barely a ripple animates the surface of the 40,000-acre lake.

Crescent Rolls

PREP 30 minutes **RISE** 2 hours 30 minutes
BAKE 8 minutes **STAND** 10 minutes

    2 packages active dry yeast
    ½ cup warm water (105° to 115°)
    1 cup milk
    1 cup instant mashed potato flakes
    ½ cup packed brown sugar
    ½ cup butter, softened
    1 teaspoon salt
    2 eggs
    2 cups whole wheat flour
    2 cups all-purpose flour
       Butter or margarine, melted

1. In a small bowl, dissolve yeast in the water. In a microwave-safe bowl, heat milk through (scald), about 1½ minutes on high.

2. In a large mixing bowl, combine milk, potato flakes, brown sugar, butter and salt. Beat with an electric mixer fitted with a dough hook on low speed for 30 seconds, scraping sides of bowl. Beat in yeast mixture and eggs until combined. Add whole wheat flour; beat on low for 3 minutes. Add 1½ cups of the all-purpose flour and beat on low for 3 minutes. Beat in enough of the remaining ½ cup flour to make a soft dough that just starts to pull away from sides of bowl (dough will be slightly sticky). Or, on lightly floured surface, knead in enough of the remaining ½ cup flour to make a moderately soft dough that is smooth and elastic (5 to 8 minutes).

3. Place dough in a lightly greased bowl; turn once. Cover; let rise in warm place until double in size (about 1½ hours).

4. Punch dough down. Turn dough out onto a lightly floured surface. Divide dough into three portions. Cover; let rest for 10 minutes. Meanwhile, lightly grease large baking sheets.

5. Roll each dough portion into a 12-inch circle. Cut each circle into eight wedges. Loosely roll each wedge toward the point, curving ends inward to form crescent. Place rolls 2 to 3 inches apart on prepared sheets. Cover and let rise in a warm place until nearly double in size (about 1 hour).

6. Bake in a 350° oven for 8 to 10 minutes or until golden. Brush tops of hot rolls with melted butter. Serve warm. **Makes 24 rolls.**

Per roll: 151 cal, 6 g fat, 29 mg chol, 154 mg sodium, 22 g carbo, 2 g fiber, 4 g pro.

Cloverleaf Rolls

PREP 1 hour **RISE** 1 hour 30 minutes
STAND 10 minutes **BAKE** 12 minutes

    1 tablespoon active dry yeast
    1 teaspoon sugar
    ¼ cup warm water (105° to 115°)
    ¾ cup milk
    ½ cup butter, cut up and softened
    ¼ cup sugar
    1 teaspoon salt
    4 to 4½ cups all-purpose flour
    2 eggs

1. In a bowl, dissolve yeast and 1 teaspoon sugar in the water. Let stand until foamy. In a microwave-safe bowl, heat milk through (scald), about 1½ minutes on high.

2. In a large mixing bowl, combine milk, butter, ¼ cup sugar and the salt. Add 1¼ cups of the flour to milk mixture. Beat with an electric mixer on low to medium speed for 30 seconds, scraping sides of bowl constantly. Beat on high speed for 3 minutes. Beat in eggs and yeast mixture. Add 1½ cups of the flour. Beat until combined. Add enough of the remaining all-purpose flour to make a soft dough that pulls from sides of the bowl.

3. On a lightly floured surface, knead in enough of the remaining flour to make a moderately stiff dough that is smooth and elastic (6 to 8 minutes). Shape dough into a ball. Place in a lightly greased bowl; turn once. Cover; let rise in a warm place until double in size (1 to 1½ hours).

4. Punch dough down. Turn dough out onto a lightly floured surface. Divide dough in half. Cover; let rest 10 minutes. Lightly grease twenty-four 2½-inch muffin cups.

5. Divide each half of the dough into 36 equal pieces. Shape each piece into a ball, pulling edges under for a smooth top. Place three balls into each prepared muffin cup, smooth side up. Cover with parchment paper; let rise in a warm place until nearly double in size (about 30 minutes).

6. Bake in a 375° oven for 12 to 15 minutes or until golden. Remove rolls from cups. Cool slightly on wire racks; serve warm. **Makes 24 rolls.**

Per roll: 130 cal, 5 g fat, 26 mg chol, 141 mg sodium, 19 g carbo, 1 g fiber, 3 g pro.

CRESCENT
ROLLS

CLOVERLEAF
ROLLS

Sparkling Basil Lemonade

The sweetness of basil and a spike of heat from fresh jalapeño infuse this refreshing summer drink.

PREP 15 minutes **COOK** 20 minutes
CHILL 2 hours

    4 cups water
    3 cups sugar
    2 cups fresh basil leaves (about 1½ ounces)
    2 1-liter bottles club soda, chilled
    2 cups lemon juice
      Ice cubes
    1 fresh jalapeño chile pepper, sliced (see
        note, page 28)
      Fresh basil leaves

1. For basil syrup: In a large saucepan, combine the water, sugar and 2 cups basil leaves. Bring to boiling over medium-high heat. Reduce heat. Simmer, uncovered, for 20 minutes. Strain and discard leaves. Cover and chill syrup for 2 to 24 hours.

2. For lemonade: In a very large punch bowl, combine chilled syrup, club soda and lemon juice. Serve over ice and garnish with jalapeño slices and fresh basil leaves. **Makes 16 servings.**

Per serving: 155 cal, 0 g fat, 0 mg chol, 29 mg sodium, 40 g carbo, 0 g fiber, 0 g pro.

Choose-a-Fruit Salsa

Play with the ingredients you have on hand. Mix two fruits. Try basil, mint or cilantro for the herb; choose red onion, green onion, chives, jalapeño and/or sweet peppers for savory crunch.

PREP 20 minutes **CHILL** 30 minutes

    3 cups finely chopped fruits
    2 tablespoons snipped fresh herb
    2 tablespoons finely chopped onion and/or
        finely chopped pepper
    1 teaspoon lime or lemon zest
    2 tablespoons lime or lemon juice
    1 tablespoon honey or sugar
    ½ teaspoon sea salt or kosher salt

In a medium bowl, toss fruits, herb, onion, citrus zest and juice, honey and salt. Cover and chill for 30 minutes (or up to 24 hours). Stir before serving with chips or over grilled meat or fish. **Makes about 3 cups.**

Per 2 tablespoons: 12 cal, 0 g fat, 0 mg chol, 34 mg sodium, 3 g carbo, 0 g fiber, 0 g pro.

Strawberry-Goat Cheese Bruschetta

PREP 15 minutes **BROIL** 4 minutes

    1 8-ounce baguette
    1 tablespoon olive oil
    1 4-ounce log goat cheese (chèvre)
    1½ cups sliced strawberries
    ½ cup arugula
      Olive oil
      Sea salt or coarse salt
      Freshly ground black pepper
      Snipped fresh herbs

1. Heat broiler. Halve baguette crosswise, then lengthwise. Place, cut sides up, on large baking sheet. Brush with the 1 tablespoon oil. Broil, 3 to 4 inches from heat, for 1½ to 2 minutes or until lightly toasted.

2. Slice and divide cheese among toasts. Top with sliced berries. Broil 2 to 3 minutes or until cheese and berries soften. Remove from broiler; top with arugula. Drizzle with additional oil. Sprinkle with salt, pepper and herbs. **Makes 4 servings.**

Per serving: 346 cal, 16 g fat, 22 mg chol, 616 mg sodium, 37 g carbo, 2 g fiber, 13 g pro.

For the best strawberries, seek out a pick-your-own patch in late May or early June. Perfectly ripe strawberries are red all of the way through, juicy, and wonderfully sweet and fragrant. Your only challenge will be stopping before you pick more than you can use.

STRAWBERRY-GOAT CHEESE
BRUSCHETTA

Mediterranean Eight-Layer Dip

PREP 45 minutes **BAKE** 25 minutes

Hummus (recipe follows)*
Tapenade (recipe follows)
2 medium tomatoes, seeded and chopped
1 cup seeded and chopped cucumber
3 tablespoons snipped fresh Italian (flat-
    leaf) parsley or curly parsley
4 teaspoons snipped fresh mint
2 teaspoons lemon juice
⅛ teaspoon kosher salt
⅛ teaspoon coarsely ground black pepper
12 large pita bread rounds
2 cups shredded fresh spinach
4 ounces feta or soft goat cheese (chèvre),
    crumbled or cut up (1 cup)
¼ cup sliced green onions (2)
¼ cup sliced or chopped pitted kalamata
    olives or pitted ripe olives

1. Prepare the Hummus and Tapenade; set aside along with remaining chopped roasted red sweet peppers (about ¾ cup).

2. In a medium bowl, toss together the tomatoes, cucumber, parsley, mint, lemon juice, salt and black pepper; set aside. Wrap pita rounds in foil and heat in a 350° oven for 15 minutes or until warm.

3. To assemble dip, spread Hummus on a 12-inch serving platter with sides; arrange spinach over Hummus layer, leaving a 1-inch border of Hummus. Drain the excess liquid from Tapenade, if needed. Spoon Tapenade over the spinach, leaving a 1-inch border.

4. Drain and discard excess liquid from tomato mixture. Spoon tomato mixture over Tapenade layer, leaving a 1-inch border. Sprinkle feta over tomato mixture. Top with reserved ¾ cup chopped roasted red sweet peppers, the green onions and olives. To serve, cut the warm pita rounds into wedges. Serve with the dip. **Makes 12 to 14 appetizer servings.**

Hummus: Drain and rinse one 15- or 16-ounce can garbanzo beans (chickpeas). In a food processor, combine garbanzo beans; ¼ cup tahini (sesame paste) or 3 tablespoons creamy peanut butter plus 1 tablespoon sesame oil; 3 tablespoons lemon juice; 2 tablespoons olive oil; 2 cloves garlic, minced; ½ teaspoon paprika; ¼ teaspoon salt; and ¼ teaspoon ground cumin. Cover and process until the mixture is smooth, stopping and scraping the sides as necessary. (Or place drained garbanzo beans in a medium bowl; mash with a potato masher or fork until nearly smooth; stir in tahini or peanut butter plus sesame oil, lemon juice, olive oil, garlic, paprika, salt and cumin.) Makes 1½ cups.

Tapenade: Drain one 12-ounce jar roasted red sweet peppers. Pat dry with paper towel. Measure ½ cup red sweet peppers to use in the tapenade. Chop the remaining red sweet peppers to use for one of the layers in dip; cover and refrigerate. In a food processor, combine the ½ cup drained red sweet peppers, ½ cup pitted kalamata olives or pitted ripe olives, ½ cup pimiento-stuffed green olives, 2 tablespoons olive oil, 1 tablespoon snipped fresh basil, 1 tablespoon drained capers, 1 teaspoon snipped fresh oregano and ¼ teaspoon freshly ground black pepper. Cover and process with several on-off turns until coarsely chopped. (Or coarsely chop red sweet peppers, olives and capers by hand. Stir in the oil, basil, oregano and black pepper.) Makes 1⅓ cups.

***For quicker prep:** Substitute 1½ cups purchased hummus for the Hummus. Assemble as directed.

Make-ahead directions: Prepare the Hummus and Tapenade as far as a week ahead, then cover and chill the mixtures until ready to assemble. Prepare tomato mixture 6 to 24 hours ahead; cover and chill until ready to assemble. Drain as directed above. Cover and chill the assembled dip up to 1 hour before serving.

Per serving: 319 cal, 11 g fat, 8 mg chol, 773 mg sodium, 47 g carbo, 5 g fiber, 10 g pro.

The 2.5-mile hike to Montreal Falls on the Upper Peninsula of Michigan ends at Lake Superior. The hike snakes through mature forest awash in thimbleberry plants. Michigan's UP has more than 320 waterfalls, many of them off the beaten path but worth the time and effort to get there.

Blue Cheese-Stuffed Burgers with Red Onion and Spinach

START TO FINISH 28 minutes

      1 pound ground beef
      1 tablespoon Worcestershire sauce
      1 teaspoon freshly ground black pepper
    ⅓ to ½ cup crumbled blue cheese (2 ounces)
      1 medium red onion, sliced crosswise
        Olive oil
      4 hamburger buns, split
      1 cup fresh baby spinach

1. In a bowl, combine beef, Worcestershire sauce and black pepper. On waxed paper, shape into eight thin 4-inch-diameter patties. Place 1 tablespoon of the blue cheese in center of four of the patties. Top with remaining four patties; pinch edges to seal.

2. Brush onion slices with olive oil; sprinkle with salt.

3. Place burgers and onions directly over medium-high heat. Grill 5 minutes per side or until no pink remains in burger. Brush cut sides of buns with olive oil. Grill, cut sides down, the last minute of grilling.

4. Serve burgers on buns with grilled onions, spinach and remaining cheese. **Makes 4 servings.**

Per serving: 497 cal, 31 g fat, 89 mg chol, 638 mg sodium, 26 g carb, 2 g fiber, 27 g pro.

Porketta

This moist pork roast preps quickly then grills slowly as the flavors of the herbs inside work their way throughout the meat, leaving a blast of Italian flavor.

PREP 20 minutes   **GRILL** 1½ hours   **STAND** 30 minutes

      2 tablespoons snipped fresh parsley
      1 teaspoon fennel seeds, crushed
      1 teaspoon minced dried onion
    ½ teaspoon dried rosemary, crushed
    ½ teaspoon dried oregano, crushed
    ¼ teaspoon salt
    ¼ teaspoon garlic powder
    ¼ teaspoon ground cloves
    ⅛ teaspoon ground coriander
      1 3- to 4-pound boneless pork top loin roast
        (double loin, tied)

1. In a small bowl, stir together parsley, fennel seeds, dried onion, rosemary, oregano, salt, garlic powder, cloves and coriander. Untie roast; sprinkle half the seasoning mixture over inside surfaces of roast. Tie up roast, using 100-percent-cotton string. Rub remaining seasoning on outside of roast.

2. To grill the roast: For a gas grill, preheat the grill. Reduce heat to medium. Adjust for indirect cooking. Place pork on grill rack over burner that is turned off. Cover and grill for 1½ to 2¼ hours or until thermometer registers 150°. (For charcoal grill, arrange medium-hot coals around a drip pan. Test for medium heat above pan. Place pork on grill rack over pan. Grill as directed, adding more coals as necessary to maintain temperature.)

3. Remove pork. Cover and let stand for 15 minutes. The temperature of meat after standing should be 160°. Transfer meat to a warm platter. Cover and let stand for 15 minutes more before carving. **Makes 9 to 12 servings.**

Per serving: 225 cal, 11 g fat, 87 mg chol, 129 mg sodium, 0 g carbo, 0 g fiber, 29 g pro.

PORKETTA

Spice-Rubbed Grilled Pork Chops on a Stick

Paul Bernhard of Bancroft, Iowa, is known as Mr. Pork Chop to thousands of hungry bicyclists who ride across the state of Iowa each summer on an annual ride. This recipe is inspired by his famous pork chop on a stick.

PREP 10 minutes **SOAK** 30 minutes **GRILL** 30 minutes **STAND** 3 minutes

    6 8x¼-inch wooden skewers, dowels or
         bamboo chopsticks
    1 teaspoon paprika
    1 teaspoon packed brown sugar
    ½ teaspoon onion salt
    ¼ teaspoon garlic powder
    ¼ teaspoon ground ginger
    ¼ teaspoon ground cinnamon
    ¼ teaspoon ground cumin
    ¼ teaspoon dry mustard
    ¼ teaspoon cayenne pepper
    ¼ teaspoon freshly cracked black pepper
    6 boneless pork top loin chops, cut 1¼ to
         1½ inches thick
    1 tablespoon soy sauce or teriyaki sauce

1. To prevent wooden skewers from burning while grilling chops, soak them in water for 30 minutes before inserting into chops.

2. For rub: In a small bowl, combine paprika, brown sugar, onion salt, garlic powder, ginger, cinnamon, cumin, mustard, cayenne and black pepper. Brush chops on both sides with soy sauce. Sprinkle rub over chops and rub in with your fingers. Insert a wooden skewer into narrow edge of each chop.

3. For a charcoal grill, arrange medium-hot coals around a drip pan. Test for medium heat above pan. Place pork chops on grill rack over pan. Cover; grill chops 30 to 35 minutes or until chops are slightly pink in center and juices run clear (145° to 160°). (For a gas grill, preheat grill. Reduce heat to medium. Adjust for indirect cooking. Place chops on grill rack over burner that is off. Cover and grill as directed.) Remove from grill; let stand for 3 minutes before serving. **Makes 6 servings.**

Per serving: 291 cal, 15 g fat, 117 mg chol, 343 mg sodium, 2 g carbo, 0 g fiber, 36 g pro.

Easy Balsamic Chicken

PREP 10 minutes **MARINATE** 1 hour
GRILL 10 minutes

    4 skinless, boneless chicken breast halves
         (about 1 pound total)
    ¼ cup balsamic vinegar
    ¼ cup olive oil
    3 cloves garlic, minced
    ¼ teaspoon salt
    ¼ teaspoon crushed red pepper

1. Place each chicken breast between two pieces of plastic wrap. Pound each lightly with the flat side of a meat mallet to make an even thickness (about ½ inch). Remove the plastic wrap.

2. Place the chicken in a shallow dish. In a small bowl or small glass measure, stir together the remaining ingredients and pour over the chicken. Cover and marinate for 1 to 4 hours.

3. Place chicken on the rack of an uncovered grill directly over medium coals. Grill, uncovered, for 10 to 12 minutes or until an instant-read thermometer registers 170° in thickest part, turning once and brushing the chicken with marinade halfway through grilling time. Discard remaining marinade. **Makes 4 servings.**

Per serving: 172 cal, 6 g fat, 66 mg chol, 123 mg sodium, 1 g carbo, 0 g fiber, 26 g pro.

EASY BALSAMIC
CHICKEN

CHICKEN, TOMATO
AND CUCUMBER
DINNER SALAD

Chicken, Tomato and Cucumber Dinner Salad

START TO FINISH 20 minutes

    5 tablespoons olive oil
    1 to 1¼ pounds chicken breast tenders
       Salt and freshly ground black pepper
    ¼ cup cider vinegar or white wine vinegar
    1 tablespoon snipped fresh thyme
    1 teaspoon sugar
    1 medium cucumber, cut in thin ribbons
    ¼ teaspoon salt
    ¼ teaspoon ground black pepper
    2 tomatoes, sliced
    ½ cup pitted green olives, halved or sliced
    4 ounces feta cheese (optional)

1. In a large skillet, heat 1 tablespoon of the olive oil over medium heat. Lightly sprinkle chicken tenders with salt and pepper. Cook chicken in hot oil for 8 to 10 minutes, turning once, until no pink remains.

2. For vinaigrette: In screw-top jar, combine remaining oil, the vinegar, thyme, sugar, salt and pepper; shake to combine.

3. Arrange chicken, cucumber ribbons, sliced tomatoes, olives and, if you like, feta cheese on plates. Drizzle vinaigrette over salads. **Makes 4 servings.**

Per serving: 336 cal, 3 g fat, 73 mg chol, 569 mg sodium, 7 g carbo, 2 g fiber, 25 g pro.

Smoky Rub

This quick rub adds triple the zing to any meat or seafood.

START TO FINISH 5 minutes

    2 teaspoons smoked sea salt*
    2 teaspoons smoked paprika*
    1 to 2 teaspoons chipotle (smoked)
       chile powder*
    2 teaspoons packed brown sugar
    2 teaspoons dried thyme, crushed
    ½ teaspoon dry mustard

1. Combine all ingredients.

2. Use 2 to 3 teaspoons per pound of meat or seafood. Rub over surface; let stand 15 to 30 minutes. Grill or broil as you like. Store unused portion for up to 1 month. **Makes about 3 tablespoons.**

*Note: Available at specialty stores or at thespicehouse.com. It's still a smokin' good rub if you substitute nonsmoked versions of one or two spices to save money.

Native plants such as bee balm (left) and switchgrass (right) are easy to maintain, inexpensive and help to add a sense of place in the Midwestern garden.

SEASONAL
PIZZETTES

Seasonal Pizzettes

One of the truest pleasures of summer—sweet, juicy, ripe, in-season tomatoes—star in these super-simple flatbreads.

PREP 20 minutes **BAKE** 10 minutes

Roasted Summer Vegetable Puree (recipe follows)
6 6- to 7-inch whole wheat or white pita bread rounds
4 ounces smoked mozzarella, thinly sliced
3 large assorted garden heirloom tomatoes, such as Black Prince, Green Zebra, Sun Gold, Cherokee Purple and/or Brandywine, or regular tomatoes, cut into ¼-inch-thick slices
4 ounces plain feta cheese or feta cheese with garlic and herbs, crumbled (1 cup)

1. Make Roasted Summer Vegetable Puree. Line two large baking sheets with foil; place pitas on baking sheets. Bake in a 400° oven for 5 to 7 minutes or until light brown. Spread tops of pitas with the vegetable puree. Top with mozzarella cheese, tomatoes and feta. Return baking sheet to oven.

2. Bake for 5 to 7 minutes more or until cheese softens and tomatoes are heated through. Cut into wedges. Serve warm or at room temperature. **Makes 6 servings.**

Roasted Summer Vegetable Puree: In a large bowl, combine 2 cups coarsely chopped peeled tomatoes (4 medium), 1 cup coarsely chopped onion (1 large), 1 cup coarsely chopped green sweet pepper (1 large), ¼ cup pickled hot banana peppers (also called Hungarian yellow wax hot chile peppers); ¾ teaspoon sea salt or kosher salt; ¾ teaspoon ground coriander; and ¾ teaspoon ground cumin. Add 2 tablespoons olive oil; toss to coat. Spread vegetable mixture evenly in a 15x10x1-inch baking pan. Roast, uncovered, in a 400° oven for 30 minutes, stirring once. Stir ¼ cup peeled garlic cloves into the vegetable mixture. Return to oven. Roast 20 minutes more or until the garlic is soft and the other vegetables are charred, stirring once. Remove from oven; let cool slightly. Transfer vegetable mixture to a medium bowl. Using an immersion blender, blend until mixture is a chunky puree. (Or transfer vegetable mixture to a food processor. Cover and pulse with several on/off turns until mixture is a chunky puree.) If needed, stir in 2 to 3 tablespoons water to get a spreadable consistency. At this point, you can cover and chill mixture up to 24 hours. Before using, stir 2 tablespoons snipped fresh basil into vegetable puree.

Per serving: 292 cal, 10 g fat, 32 mg chol, 674 mg sodium, 40 g carbo, 6 g fiber, 14 g pro.

Gnocchi, Sweet Corn and Arugula in Cream Sauce

START TO FINISH 20 minutes

12 ounces frozen or shelf-stable potato gnocchi
2 small ears fresh sweet corn or 2 cups frozen whole kernel corn
1 cup half-and-half
1 3-ounce package cream cheese, cut up
½ teaspoon each salt, garlic powder and dried basil or oregano
¼ teaspoon freshly ground black pepper
3 cups torn fresh arugula
Crushed red pepper (optional)

1. In Dutch oven, cook gnocchi according to package directions, adding corn the last 5 minutes of cooking time. Use tongs to transfer ears of corn (if using) to cutting board. Drain gnocchi and corn kernels (if using), reserving ½ cup of the pasta water. Do not rinse.

2. Meanwhile, for cream sauce, in a medium saucepan, combine half-and-half, cream cheese, salt, garlic powder, dried herb and pepper. Cook over medium heat for 10 minutes, stirring frequently. Stir in reserved pasta water. Return cooked pasta to Dutch oven. Cut corn from cob and add to pasta. Pour cream sauce over pasta; heat through, if necessary. Stir in arugula. Serve in bowls. Sprinkle with additional salt, pepper, dried herb and, if you like, crushed red pepper. **Makes 4 servings.**

Per serving: 328 cal, 13 g fat, 40 mg chol, 908 mg sodium, 46 g carbo, 1 g fiber, 8 g pro.

Garden Vegetable Tart

START TO FINISH 34 minutes

1 frozen puff pastry sheet (half of a
    17.3-ounce package)
2 ears of fresh sweet corn
1 medium zucchini, thinly sliced lengthwise
1 pint cherry tomatoes
1 tablespoon extra-virgin olive oil
½ teaspoon salt
¼ cup tomato paste
¼ cup water
4 ounces fresh mozzarella, thinly sliced
    Crushed red pepper and dried basil
    (optional)

1. On a lightly floured surface, roll puff pastry to a 14x10-inch rectangle; transfer to a 15x10x1-inch baking pan. Prick pastry all over with a fork. Bake in a 425° oven about 10 minutes or until center is set. Remove from oven; lightly press center with a spatula.

2. Meanwhile, wrap husked and cleaned corn in waxed paper. Microwave on 100% power (high) for 2 minutes. Brush corn, zucchini and tomatoes with 1 tablespoon olive oil; sprinkle with the salt. Preheat an indoor grill pan over medium-high heat. Grill vegetables until tender, 5 to 7 minutes, turning occasionally. Transfer to platter; cover and keep warm.

3. In a small bowl, whisk together tomato paste and the water; spread on puff pastry. Cut corn from cobs. Top pastry with cheese and vegetables. Bake tart 10 minutes, until pastry is golden and cheese is melted. Top with red pepper and basil, if you like.

Makes 4 servings.

Per serving: 454 cal, 29 g fat, 20 mg chol, 750 mg sodium, 38 g carbo, 3 g fiber, 11 g pro.

Midwest gardens and farmers markets are bursting with bright, beautiful at-peak produce this time of year. Eating fresh is easy!

Boston Lettuce Stacks with Grilled Peaches, Feta and Pecans

To concentrate their flavor, cook peaches on your grill for this easy summer salad.

PREP 15 minutes **GRILL** 8 minutes

⅓ cup bottled light balsamic vinaigrette
   salad dressing
 2 tablespoons orange juice or apple juice
 1 tablespoon honey
 1 teaspoon finely snipped fresh chives or
   green onion
 4 ripe peaches or small pears
16 Boston lettuce or Bibb lettuce leaves
   (about 2 heads)
¼ cup broken pecans or walnuts, toasted
¼ cup dried cherries, dried cranberries
   and/or golden raisins; or ½ cup fresh
   raspberries or sliced strawberries
 1 ounce feta cheese, semisoft goat cheese
   (chèvre) or blue cheese, crumbled (¼ cup)
   Freshly ground black pepper (optional)

1. In a screw-top jar, combine the vinaigrette, orange juice, honey and chives. Cover and shake well.

2. Cut peaches in half lengthwise; remove pits. (If using pears, halve lengthwise and core.) Brush cut sides of fruit with some of the vinaigrette mixture.

3. For a gas or charcoal grill, grill peach halves, cut sides down, on the rack of a covered grill directly over medium heat for 8 to 10 minutes or until lightly browned and warmed through, flipping over once halfway through grilling.

4. To serve, stack four of the lettuce leaves on each of four chilled salad plates. Drizzle with the remaining vinaigrette mixture. Slice fruit into wedges or quarters and remove peel, if you like; arrange on lettuce. Sprinkle with pecans, cherries and feta. If you like, sprinkle with pepper. Serve immediately. **Makes 4 servings.**

*Tip: To toast nuts on grill, place pecans or walnuts in a small cast-iron skillet on the grill rack. Toast over medium heat for 5 to 7 minutes. (Or toast in baking pan in 350° oven for 5 to 10 minutes.)

Per serving: 189 cal, 8 g fat, 6 mg chol, 275 mg sodium, 32 g carbo, 4 g fiber, 4 g pro.

Up to 100 vendors sell their goods at the farmers market in Athens, Ohio, every Wednesday and Saturday year-round.

Fresh Corn Cakes with Garden Relish

PREP 30 minutes **COOK** 5 minutes + 4 minutes per batch

2 cups fresh corn kernels
½ cup chopped sweet onion
2 tablespoons olive oil
1 cup buttermilk
1 egg, lightly beaten
¾ cup quick-cooking polenta mix
½ cup all-purpose flour
1¼ teaspoons baking powder
¾ teaspoon baking soda
½ teaspoon salt
    Garden Relish (recipe follows)
    Fresh basil leaves (optional)

1. In a skillet, cook and stir corn and onion in 1 tablespoon of the oil over medium-high heat 5 minutes or until onion is tender. Remove from heat; cool. Place half of the corn mixture in a food processor. Cover; process until nearly smooth. Transfer to a bowl. Stir in buttermilk and egg.

2. In another bowl, stir together polenta mix, flour, baking powder, baking soda and salt. Add polenta mixture to buttermilk mixture; stir just until combined. Stir in remaining corn mixture.

3. In a very large skillet, heat the remaining 1 tablespoon oil over medium heat. For each cake, pour about ¼ cup batter into the hot skillet; spread batter if necessary. Cook over medium heat about 2 minutes per side or until golden. Add more oil to skillet as needed. To serve, spoon Garden Relish on corn cakes and, if you like, top with basil. **Makes 6 (2 cake) servings.**

Garden Relish: In a bowl, combine 1 seeded and chopped red sweet pepper, 1½ cups corn kernels, ½ cup chopped onion and ¼ cup chopped basil. Stir in 1 tablespoon olive oil. Add salt and black pepper to taste.

Per serving: 352 cal, 9 g fat, 37 mg chol, 558 mg sodium, 61 g carbo, 7 g fiber, 10 g pro.

There are no electronics in sight—just the simple summer ritual of catching some air off of a dock before splashing down into the cooling waters of a lake.

Fresh Corn Salad

If corn is less than perfect, you can refresh it: Blanch 1 minute in boiling salted water, then transfer to salted ice water to stop cooking.

START TO FINISH 35 minutes

½ cup cider vinegar
¼ to ⅓ cup sugar
1 teaspoon kosher salt
½ teaspoon coarsely ground black pepper
4 ears fresh corn
½ cup finely diced red onion (cut to same size as the corn kernels), soaked in ice water for 20 minutes and patted dry
½ cup cucumber, seeded but not peeled (if unwaxed), diced to same size as onions
½ cup red or orange sweet pepper, diced to same size as onions
½ cup cherry or pear tomatoes, halved or quartered
3 tablespoons parsley, finely torn
1 tablespoon basil leaves or buds, pulled apart
1 tablespoon fresh jalapeño, seeds and veins removed, very finely diced (see note, page 28)
½ teaspoon sea salt or kosher salt
1 to 2 cups small arugula leaves

1. For dressing: In a glass bowl, whisk together vinegar, sugar, 1 teaspoon kosher salt and the black pepper until sugar is dissolved. Allow dressing to stand while preparing salad.

2. For the salad: cut corn kernels from cobs. In a large bowl, toss the corn and all remaining ingredients except the sea salt and arugula leaves.

3. At serving time, transfer corn mixture to a serving bowl. Season with the ½ teaspoon sea salt. Add the dressing and arugula leaves. Serve immediately. (The cucumbers and tomatoes will begin to break down.)
Makes 8 servings.

Per serving: 77 cal, 1 g fat, 401 mg sodium, 17 g carbo, 2 g fiber, 2 g pro.

It's called orange butterfly milkweed for a reason. The native prairie plant erupts in juicy reddish-orange blossoms in early summer and attracts monarchs and hummingbirds.

Cyclists travel through some of North Dakota's most scenic spots on the 120-mile Maah Daah Hey Trail. The trail runs through the historic town of Medora—one-time home of Teddy Roosevelt. At nearby Teddy Roosevelt National Park, herds of wild mustangs, bison, elk and pronghorn antelope roam freely.

PEANUT BUTTER
OATMEAL BIGGIES

Peanut Butter Oatmeal Biggies

Sandwich your choice of ice cream between our chewy, saucer-size cookies for a make-ahead treat. If you're a chocolate chip fan, substitute them for part or all of the raisins.

PREP 10 minutes **BAKE** 10 minutes **STAND** 1 minute

¾ cup peanut butter
½ cup butter, softened
¾ cup packed brown sugar
½ cup granulated sugar
½ teaspoon baking powder
¼ teaspoon baking soda
2 eggs
1 teaspoon vanilla
1¼ cups all-purpose flour
2½ cups regular rolled oats
1½ cups raisins and/or semisweet chocolate pieces
Ice cream (optional)

1. Lightly grease large cookie sheets; set aside. In a large mixing bowl, beat peanut butter and butter on low to medium speed with electric mixer for 30 seconds. Add the brown and granulated sugars, baking powder and baking soda to mixing bowl. Beat until mixture is fluffy.

2. Add eggs and vanilla; beat until combined. Beat in the flour. With a wooden spoon, stir in rolled oats and raisins.

3. Using ¼ cup dough for each cookie, drop dough 3 inches apart on greased cookie sheets. Press into 4-inch circles.

4. Bake in 375° oven 10 to 12 minutes or until edges are golden. Let cookies stand 1 minute on cookie sheets. Transfer cookies to wire racks to cool. Sandwich with ice cream, if you like. **Makes 16 to 18 large cookies.**

Per cookie with raisins: 318 cal, 14 g fat, 42 mg chol, 137 mg sodium, 46 g carbo, 3 g fiber, 7 g pro.

Whoopie Pie Cake

(Pictured on page 87.)

PREP 50 minutes **STAND** 30 minutes **BAKE** 1 hour **COOL** 1 hour

1½ cups butter, softened
5 eggs
1 tablespoon unsweetened cocoa powder
1 tablespoon butter, melted
1¼ cups unsweetened cocoa powder
2 cups all-purpose flour
¼ cup buttermilk powder
1 teaspoon baking powder
1 teaspoon salt
½ teaspoon baking soda
2½ cups packed brown sugar
1 tablespoon vanilla
½ teaspoon instant-coffee crystals
1 cup water
Marshmallow Filling (recipe follows)
Chocolate Glaze (recipe follows)

1. Allow the 1½ cups butter and the eggs to stand at room temperature for 30 minutes. In a small bowl, make a paste of 1 tablespoon cocoa powder and 1 tablespoon melted butter. Coat a 10-inch fluted tube pan with the paste; set aside.

2. For cake: In a medium bowl, stir together the 1¼ cups cocoa, the flour, buttermilk powder, baking powder, salt and baking soda. Set aside. In a large mixing bowl, beat butter with an electric mixer on medium to high speed for 30 seconds. Gradually add brown sugar, beating about 5 minutes or until light and fluffy. Beat in vanilla and coffee crystals. Add eggs, one at a time, beating 1 minute after each addition and scraping bowl frequently. Add one-third of the cocoa mixture and ½ cup of the water, beating on low speed just until combined. Repeat. Add remaining one-third of the cocoa mixture, beating about 30 seconds or until smooth. Spread batter in prepared pan.

3. Bake in a 325° oven about 1 hour or until a toothpick inserted near the center comes out clean. Cool in pan on wire rack for 10 minutes. Remove cake from pan; cool on wire rack.

4. Split cake in half horizontally. Spread Marshmallow Filling on the bottom half of cake. Replace top on Marshmallow Filling. Drizzle Chocolate Glaze over cake. **Makes 16 servings.**

Marshmallow Filling: In a large mixing bowl, beat ¾ cup softened butter with an electric mixer on medium speed until smooth. Add one 7-ounce jar marshmallow crème, 1½ cups powdered sugar and 1½ teaspoons vanilla. Beat until smooth.

Chocolate Glaze: In a small saucepan, heat ¼ cup whipping cream over medium heat. Add ⅓ cup semisweet chocolate pieces. Heat and stir over low heat until melted and smooth.

Per serving: 586 cal, 32 g fat, 134 mg chol, 498 mg sodium, 74 g carbo, 3 g fiber, 6 g pro.

Coconut Cake

PREP 50 minutes **STAND** 30 minutes **BAKE** 22 minutes **COOL** 1 hour

5 eggs
½ cup butter
2 cups all-purpose flour
1 teaspoon baking soda
½ teaspoon salt
½ cup shortening
2 cups sugar
1 teaspoon vanilla
1 cup buttermilk
1⅔ cups shredded coconut
½ cup chopped pecans
Cream Cheese Frosting (recipe follows)
1 cup shredded coconut
½ cup chopped pecans
Shredded coconut
Pecan halves

1. Separate eggs. Allow egg yolks, egg whites and butter to stand at room temperature for 30 minutes. Meanwhile, grease and flour three 9x1½-inch cake pans. In a medium bowl, stir together flour, baking soda and salt; set aside.

2. In a large mixing bowl, beat butter and shortening with an electric mixer on medium to high speed for 30 seconds. Gradually add sugar, beating on medium speed until light and fluffy (4 to 5 minutes), scraping sides of bowl occasionally. Add egg yolks, one at a time, beating well after each addition. Beat in vanilla. Alternately add flour mixture and buttermilk, beating on low speed after each addition just until combined. Stir in 1⅔ cups coconut and ½ cup pecans.

3. Wash beaters. In a medium mixing bowl, beat egg whites on medium to high speed until stiff peaks form (tips stand straight). Gently fold one-third of the beaten egg whites into batter. Fold in remaining egg whites. Spread batter evenly in prepared pans.

4. Bake in a 350° oven for 22 to 28 minutes or until a toothpick inserted in centers comes out clean. Cool layers in pans on wire racks for 10 minutes. Remove from pans; cool on wire racks.

5. To assemble, spread about ¾ cup of the Cream Cheese Frosting over the first cake layer. Sprinkle with ½ cup coconut and ¼ cup pecans. Add second cake layer, bottom side down. Spread with ¾ cup frosting. Sprinkle with remaining ½ cup coconut and ¼ cup pecans. Add third cake layer, bottom side up. Thinly frost cake to seal crumbs. Spread with remaining frosting. Garnish top and sides of cake with additional coconut and pecan halves. **Makes 16 servings.**

Cream Cheese Frosting: Cut one 8-ounce package cream cheese into small pieces. In a large mixing bowl, beat cream cheese pieces, ½ cup softened butter and ⅛ teaspoon salt with an electric mixer on medium speed until smooth. Gradually add 4 to 5 cups powdered sugar, ½ cup at a time, beating well after each addition, to reach spreading consistency.

Per serving: 667 cal, 38 g fat, 105 mg chol, 414 mg sodium, 78 g carbo, 3 g fiber, 7 g pro.

COCONUT CAKE
AND WHOOPIE PIE
CAKE, PAGE 85

Pistachio Pavlova with Fresh Berries

PREP 30 minutes **BAKE** 30 minutes **STAND** 1 hour 30 minutes **CHILL** 2 hours

  5 eggs
 ½ teaspoon cream of tartar
  2 teaspoons vanilla
1¼ cups sugar
 ½ teaspoon finely chopped pistachios
  1 cup whipping cream
  1 tablespoon sugar
 ½ teaspoon vanilla
  3 cups sliced fresh strawberries and/or
      raspberries
  2 cups fresh strawberries, halved, or
      raspberries
  2 to 3 tablespoons sugar

1. Separate eggs and let whites stand in a large bowl for 30 minutes. (Reserve yolks for other use.) Line a large baking sheet with parchment paper. Draw a 9x1½-inch circle on the paper. Turn paper pencil-side down; set pan aside.

2. For meringue: Beat egg whites and cream of tartar with electric mixer on medium speed for 1 minute or until soft peaks form (tips curl when beaters are lifted). Beat in 2 teaspoons vanilla. Add 1¼ cups sugar, 1 tablespoon at a time, beating after each addition until sugar dissolves. (Meringue should feel smooth.) Beat on high speed for about 7 minutes or until stiff peaks form (tips stand straight when beaters are lifted). Gently fold in nuts.

3. Using back of a spoon, fill circle on paper with meringue, forming a bowl with ½-inch-thick bottom and 2-inch sides.

4. Bake in a 300° oven for 30 to 35 minutes or until top has cracks. Turn off oven. Let meringue dry in oven, with door closed, for 1 hour. (Do not open oven.) Carefully lift shell off paper. Transfer to a wire rack; cool completely.

5. For whipped cream: In a large mixing bowl, beat whipping cream, 1 tablespoon sugar and ½ teaspoon vanilla with an electric mixer on medium speed until soft peaks form.

6. Fill "bowl" of meringue with whipped cream. Arrange 3 cups sliced strawberries on top of cream. Cover; chill 2 to 24 hours.

7. For sauce: In a blender or food processor, combine 2 cups strawberries and 2 to 3 tablespoons sugar. Cover and blend or process until smooth. Press berry mixture through a fine-mesh sieve; discard seeds. Cover and chill 2 to 24 hours.

8. To serve, spoon sauce over sliced strawberries in the shell. **Makes 8 to 10 servings.**

Per serving: 331 cal, 15 g fat, 41 mg chol, 48 mg sodium, 47 g carbo, 3 g fiber, 5 g pro.

Crisp on the outside and soft and marshmallowy on the inside, a Pavlova is like a fruit-topped cloud. It's light but sweet—a perfect ending to a hearty meal.

Cranberry Pecan Tarts

PREP 35 minutes **BAKE** 30 minutes **COOL** 10 minutes

1 tablespoon orange zest
½ cup orange juice
⅔ cup chopped dried cranberries
½ cup butter, softened
1 3-ounce package cream cheese, softened
1 cup all-purpose flour
1 egg
¾ cup packed brown sugar
1 tablespoon cornstarch
1 tablespoon butter, melted
1 teaspoon vanilla
⅛ teaspoon salt
½ cup chopped pecans

1. Set aside orange zest. In a small saucepan, bring orange juice to boiling. Add cranberries. Remove from heat; let stand for 10 minutes. Drain cranberries; discard the juice.

2. In a medium mixing bowl, beat ½ cup butter and the cream cheese with an electric mixer on medium speed until combined. Stir in flour. Divide dough into 24 balls. Press balls into the bottoms and up sides of 24 ungreased 2- to 2½-inch fluted tart pans or 1¾-inch muffin cups.

3. In a small bowl, stir together egg, brown sugar, cornstarch, orange zest, 1 tablespoon melted butter, the vanilla and salt until combined. Stir in drained cranberries and pecans. Spoon about 1 tablespoon of the filling into dough-lined pans. If using tart pans, set on cookie sheet.

4. Bake in a 325° oven about 30 minutes or until crust is golden. Cool in pan on a wire rack for 10 minutes. Remove tarts from pans by running a knife around edges. Let cool. **Makes 24 (1 tart) servings.**

Per tart: 129 cal, 7 g fat, 23 mg chol, 67 mg sodium, 15 g carbo, 1 g fiber, 1 g pro.

The setting sun creates a fiery amber canvas to enjoy from the Ferris wheel at the Iowa State Fair—a festival that celebrates hard work, lots of fun, and all kinds of tasty food on a stick.

MOLASSES COOKIES

Molasses Cookies

PREP 25 minutes **CHILL** 1 hour
BAKE 8 minutes **COOL** 2 minutes

2½ cups all-purpose flour
 2 teaspoons baking soda
 1 teaspoon ground cinnamon
 1 teaspoon ground ginger
 1 teaspoon ground nutmeg
 1 teaspoon ground allspice
 ½ teaspoon salt
 ¾ cup shortening
 1 cup packed brown sugar
 1 egg
 ½ cup molasses
 ¼ cup granulated sugar

1. In a medium bowl, stir together flour, baking soda, cinnamon, ginger, nutmeg, allspice and salt. Set aside.

2. In a large bowl, beat shortening with an electric mixer on medium speed for 30 seconds. Add brown sugar; beat until mixture is combined, scraping sides of bowl occasionally. Beat in egg and molasses until combined. Add flour mixture, beating on low speed just until mixture is combined. Cover and chill for 1 to 2 hours, until dough is easy to handle.

3. Place granulated sugar in a small bowl. Shape dough into 1-inch balls. Roll balls in sugar to coat. Place about 1½ inches apart on lightly greased cookie sheets.

4. Bake in a 350° oven for 8 to 10 minutes or until bottoms are light brown and tops are puffed. Cool on cookie sheets for 2 minutes. Transfer to wire racks and let cool. **Makes 52 cookies.**

Per cookie: 78 cal, 3 g fat, 4 mg chol, 75 mg sodium, 12 g carbo, 0 g fiber, 1 g pro.

True Butterscotch Pie

(Pictured on page 94.)

PREP 30 minutes **CHILL** at least 2 hours

    Baked Pastry Shell (recipe follows)
1¼ cups packed dark brown sugar
 ¼ cup butter
 ⅓ cup all-purpose flour
 1 teaspoon cornstarch
 2 cups whipping cream
 3 egg yolks
 3 tablespoons butter, cut up
 1 teaspoon vanilla
    Whipped Cream Topping (recipe follows)

1. Prepare Baked Pastry Shell.

2. In a medium saucepan, combine ½ cup brown sugar and ¼ cup butter. Cook and stir over low heat until butter melts and mixture is smooth. Remove from heat.

3. In a small bowl, combine the remaining ¾ cup brown sugar, the flour and cornstarch. Add flour mixture to butter mixture; stir until combined. Gradually stir in whipping cream. Return saucepan to heat. Cook and stir over medium heat until thickened and bubbly; reduce heat. Cook and stir for 2 minutes more. Remove from heat.

4. In a small bowl, lightly beat egg yolks. Gradually stir about 1 cup of the hot filling into yolks. Add yolk mixture to saucepan. Bring to a gentle boil over medium heat, stirring constantly; reduce heat. Cook and stir 2 minutes more. Remove from heat. Stir in 3 tablespoons butter and the vanilla. Pour filling into the baked shell. Cover with plastic wrap. Chill for at least 2 hours.

5. To serve, prepare Whipped Cream Topping. Spread topping evenly over cold filling. Serve immediately, or store, covered, in the refrigerator until ready to serve. **Makes 8 to 10 servings.**

Baked Pastry Shell: In a medium bowl, stir together 1¼ cups all-purpose flour and ¼ teaspoon salt. Cut in ⅓ cup shortening until pieces are pea-size. Sprinkle 1 tablespoon ice water over part of the flour mixture; toss with fork. Push moistened pastry to side of bowl. Repeat until all of the flour mixture is moistened (4 to 5 tablespoons water total). Roll dough into a 12-inch circle on a lightly floured surface. Wrap pastry around rolling pin; unroll into a 9-inch pie plate. Ease pastry into pie plate without stretching. Trim pastry to ½ inch beyond edge of pie plate. Fold under pastry even with edge of plate. Crimp as desired. Prick bottom and sides of pastry with a fork. Line pastry with a double thickness of foil. Bake in a 450° oven for 8 minutes. Remove foil. Bake for 6 to 8 minutes more or until pastry is golden brown. Cool on a wire rack.

Whipped Cream Topping: In a chilled mixing bowl, beat 1¾ cups whipping cream, ¼ cup powdered sugar and ¼ teaspoon vanilla with an electric mixer on medium speed until moderately stiff peaks form.

Per serving: 810 cal, 62 g fat, 250 mg chol, 218 mg sodium, 60 g carbo, 1 g fiber, 6 g pro.

FIRST PLACE FOOD

DES MOINES

StateFair

MIXED DRIED FRUIT PIE

TRUE BUTTERSCOTCH
PIE, PAGE 93

Mixed Dried Fruit Pie

PREP 45 minutes **BAKE** 50 minutes **COOL** 1 hour 30 minutes **CHILL** 30 minutes

4 cups water
3 cups dried apple slices
1 cup dried apricots, sliced
1 cup dried tart and/or sweet cherries
  Pastry for Double-Crust Pie (recipe follows)
¼ cup orange juice
1 teaspoon lemon zest
1 teaspoon lemon juice
¾ cup packed brown sugar
2 tablespoons all-purpose flour
1 teaspoon ground cinnamon
¼ teaspoon salt
4½ teaspoons butter, cut up
1 egg, lightly beaten
1 tablespoon water

1. In a large saucepan, bring 4 cups water, the apples, apricots and cherries to boiling; reduce heat. Simmer, uncovered, 10 minutes, stirring occasionally. Remove from heat; cool to room temperature.

2. Meanwhile, prepare Pastry for Double-Crust Pie. Halve dough. Slightly flatten each half into a 4-inch disk. Chill, covered, for no longer than 30 minutes.

3. Stir orange juice, lemon zest and lemon juice into the cooled fruit mixture. In a small bowl, combine brown sugar, flour, cinnamon and salt. Combine flour mixture and fruit mixture. Set filling aside.

4. On a lightly floured surface, roll both portions of dough into 12-inch circles. Wrap one pastry circle around rolling pin; unroll into a 9-inch pie plate without stretching. Trim pastry even with edge of pie plate. Cut slits in other pastry to allow steam to escape. If you like, use trimmed pastry pieces as decorative designs.

5. Transfer filling to the pastry-lined pie plate. Dot with butter. Place pastry circle on filling; trim pastry to ½ inch beyond edge of pie plate. Fold top pastry edge under bottom pastry. Crimp as desired. If using, decorate with pastry cutouts.

6. In a small bowl, combine beaten egg and 1 tablespoon water. Brush onto top pastry. Cover edge of pie with foil. Place foil-lined baking sheet on oven rack below pie.

7. Bake in a 375° oven for 30 minutes. Remove foil. Bake for 20 to 30 minutes more or until filling is bubbly and crust is golden (if necessary, cover top of pie with foil the last 10 to 15 minutes). Cool on a wire rack. **Makes 8 servings.**

Pastry for Double-Crust Pie: In a large bowl, stir together 2 cups all-purpose flour, 1 tablespoon sugar, 1 teaspoon salt and ½ teaspoon ground cinnamon. Using a pastry blender, cut in ¾ cup butter-flavored shortening until pieces are pea-size. In a small bowl, combine 7 tablespoons cold water and ¼ cup all-purpose flour; stir until mixture is smooth. Pour water mixture over the dry ingredients; mix with a fork until moistened. Knead to form ball.

Per serving: 606 cal, 21 g fat, 29 mg chol, 439 mg sodium, 101 g carbo, 7 g fiber, 6 g pro.

S'more Outrageous Chocolate Shakes

A cascade of chocolate syrup drizzled inside the glass adds drama to a chocolate chip cookie dough shake crowned with crushed grahams, mini chocolate chips and marshmallows.

START TO FINISH 10 minutes

1 pint chocolate chip cookie dough ice cream, chocolate ice cream or chocolate frozen yogurt

½ to ¾ cup chocolate milk or milk

3 to 4 tablespoons hot fudge-flavor ice cream topping, chocolate-hazelnut spread or peanut butter

2 tablespoons chocolate or plain malted milk powder (optional)
Chocolate-flavor syrup, chilled

2 tablespoons crushed chocolate, honey or cinnamon graham crackers

1 tablespoon miniature semisweet chocolate pieces

4 toasted coconut marshmallows or 2 tablespoons plain or flavored tiny marshmallows

1. In a blender, combine ice cream, milk, ice cream topping and, if you like, the malt powder. Cover and blend until smooth.

2. Drizzle chocolate syrup around insides of two tall glasses. Pour the shake mixture into glasses. Top each with crushed graham crackers and chocolate pieces. Garnish with coconut marshmallows. If using mini marshmallows, use a kitchen blowtorch to carefully caramelize the marshmallow tops, if you like. **Makes 2 milk shakes (about 1¼ cups each).**

Per shake: 930 cal, 48 g fat, 198 mg chol, 404 mg sodium, 112 g carbo, 2 g fiber, 13 g pro.

Kids vie for the hammocks at Still Waters Resort at Missouri's Table Rock Lake. The resort is just 2 miles from Silver Dollar City but you don't hear the bustle of Branson here, just a quiet hum.

S'more Pie à la Marshmallow Crème

Cream cheese brings body and richness to so-chocolatey mousse filling. More wow comes from the blend of marshmallow crème and crème de cacao draped over the top.

PREP 45 minutes **COOL** 20 minutes **CHILL** 4 hours

- 6 ounces chocolate, finely chopped
- ¼ cup whipping cream
- 2 tablespoons dark-color corn syrup
- ¼ cup water
- 2 teaspoons vanilla or crème de cacao
- ½ of an 8-ounce package cream cheese, softened
- 1 cup whipping cream
- ½ cup powdered sugar
- 1 cup tiny marshmallows
- Graham Cracker Crust (recipe follows)
- Topper (recipe follows)
- Crushed graham crackers (optional)
- Shaved chocolate (optional)

1. In a heavy saucepan, mix chocolate, ¼ cup cream, the corn syrup and the water. Heat and stir constantly over medium-low heat until smooth. Remove from heat; stir in vanilla. Cool 20 minutes, stirring occasionally.

2. In a bowl, mix chocolate mixture and cream cheese. In a chilled mixing bowl, beat 1 cup cream and the powdered sugar with electric mixer until soft peaks form. Using a spatula, fold the cream mixture into the chocolate mixture.

3. Place marshmallows in bottom of crust. Spoon in chocolate mixture. Cover; chill at least 4 hours or until well-chilled. Spoon on topper and, if you like, additional crushed graham crackers and shaved chocolate.

Makes 10 servings.

Graham Cracker Crust: Coat a 9-inch pie plate with cooking spray. Melt ⅓ cup butter; stir in ¼ cup sugar. Add 1¼ cups finely crushed honey, chocolate or cinnamon graham crackers; toss to mix. Press onto bottom and up sides of pie plate. Bake in 375° oven 5 minutes. Cool.

Topper: In a bowl, mix one 7-ounce jar marshmallow crème and 1 tablespoon crème de cacao or milk. If you like, stir in 1 cup tiny marshmallows.

Per serving: 511 cal, 30 g fat, 72 mg chol, 167 mg sodium, 61 g carbo, 2 g fiber, 5 g pro.

Try a twist on the time-honored s'more. Graham crackers, chocolate and marshmallow are just meant for each other—whether in the toasty campfire treat or in this chilled summertime pie.

S'MORE COOKIES

S'more Cookies

Cinnamon, brown sugar, oats and finely crushed grahams shape this moist cookie made even more irresistible with a thumbprint filling of marshmallow crème and an upside-down milk chocolate candy.

PREP 35 minutes **CHILL** 1 hour **BAKE** 10 minutes per batch

    4 cups regular rolled oats
 1½ cups all-purpose flour
    1 cup finely crushed graham crackers
    1 teaspoon baking soda
    1 teaspoon baking powder
    1 teaspoon ground cinnamon
  ½ teaspoon salt
    1 cup butter, softened
    1 cup packed brown sugar
  ½ cup granulated sugar
    2 eggs
  ¼ cup milk
    1 tablespoon vanilla
    1 7-ounce jar marshmallow crème
  42 milk chocolate Kisses

1. In a bowl, mix oats, flour, crushed graham crackers, baking soda, baking powder, cinnamon and salt. Set aside.

2. In a large bowl, beat butter with electric mixer 30 seconds. Beat in brown and granulated sugars. Beat in eggs, milk and vanilla. Beat in as much flour mixture as you can, stirring in any remaining with a wooden spoon. Chill, covered, for 1 to 4 hours.

3. Drop dough by rounded tablespoonfuls 2 inches apart onto lightly greased cookie sheets. Bake cookies in a 375° oven for 8 minutes; remove from oven.

4. Using the back of a teaspoon measure, make an indentation in each cookie top. Fill a plastic bag with marshmallow crème. Seal bag; snip off tiny corner of bag. Pipe 1 teaspoon crème into center of each cookie. Push a chocolate candy into cream, point side down. Return cookies to oven; bake 2 or 3 minutes more or until edges are light brown. Cool on cookie sheets 1 minute. Cool completely on wire racks. **Makes 42 cookies.**

Per cookie: 165 cal, 7 g fat, 23 mg chol, 134 mg sodium, 24 g carbo, 1 g fiber, 3 g pro.

S'more Chocolate and Honey Fondue

Three ingredients melt together for a grown-up dark chocolate fondue spiked with amaretto. Along with the requisite graham crackers and assorted marshmallow dunkers, get creative with fruit segments and brownie bites.

START TO FINISH 35 minutes

    1 cup half-and-half or light cream
  ¼ cup honey
    3 3.52-ounce bars Swiss dark chocolate with honey and almond nougat or 10½ ounces bittersweet or semisweet chocolate, finely chopped
    3 tablespoons amaretto, hazelnut liqueur, brandy or apricot brandy; or 3 tablespoons half-and-half and ¼ teaspoon almond extract
      Dippers: marshmallows, graham cracker snack sticks, biscotti, cake, dried apricots and/or fresh fruit dippers

1. In a heavy small saucepan, combine the half-and-half and honey. Bring mixture to a simmer over medium heat, stirring often. Reduce heat to low. Add chocolate and whisk until mixture is smooth and chocolate is melted. Remove from heat. Whisk in the amaretto.

2. Transfer the chocolate mixture to a fondue pot and keep warm over a fondue burner; stir occasionally. (Or use a 1- or 1½-quart slow cooker and keep warm for up to 2 hours on low-heat setting.)

3. Serve fondue with your choice of dippers. Spear a dipper with a fondue fork or wooden skewer; dip into chocolate mixture. (If the fondue mixture thickens, stir in a little more half-and-half to thin as needed.) **Makes 8 servings.**

Per serving: 292 cal, 14 g fat, 15 mg chol, 34 mg sodium, 35 g carbo, 1 g fiber, 3 g pro.

Walleye, northern and smallmouth bass draw anglers to Lake Vermillion in northern Minnesota, but that's not all there is to enjoy in the area. Roadside strawberry patches, a little farmers market and a charming restored 1939 movie theater in the nearby town of Cook (population: 500) all feel like discoveries.

Fresh Strawberry Bars

The rich peanut butter base can be made ahead and frozen. For individual servings, cut the base in portions and freeze. Pull a portion from the freezer, thaw, and top with jam and berries for a last-minute dessert.

PREP 25 minutes **BAKE** 25 minutes

¾ cup butter, softened
¾ cup peanut butter
1 cup packed brown sugar
½ cup granulated sugar
2 teaspoons baking powder
¼ teaspoon salt
2 eggs
1 teaspoon vanilla
2¼ cups all-purpose flour
½ cup strawberry jam
4 cups small whole strawberries, halved or quartered

1. Line 13x9x2-inch baking pan with foil, extending foil beyond edges. Set aside.

2. In a large mixing bowl, beat butter and peanut butter on medium to high speed for 30 seconds. Beat in sugars, baking powder and salt until combined. Add eggs and vanilla; beat until combined. Beat in as much flour as you can with mixer. Stir in remaining flour.

3. Spread dough in prepared pan. Bake in a 350° oven 25 minutes or until top is lightly browned and toothpick inserted near center comes out clean.

4. Cool completely on rack. Remove from pan by lifting foil. Spread jam over top; top with berries. Cut into bars. Serve at once or refrigerate up to 6 hours. **Makes 24 bars.**

Make-ahead directions: Wrap the peanut butter base in foil; store at room temperature up to 24 hours. Before serving, top with jam and berries. Or freeze the peanut butter base in a freezer container up to 3 months.

Per bar: 225 cal, 10 g fat, 33 mg chol, 143 mg sodium, 30 g carbo, 1 g fiber, 4 g pro.

An ice cream cone enhances a sunset stroll along the shore of Lake Charlevoix in Boyne City, Michigan. Boyne City has recently reinvented itself as a laid-back version of the larger shore towns on Lake Michigan, which is just 15 miles away.

FARMERS MARKET
BROWNIES

LEMON CURD TART

Farmers Market Brownies

These indulgent chocolate treats were conjured up at The Incredibly Delicious Flourless Chocolate Cake Company in Springfield, Illinois. The bakery and cafe is in an Italianate mansion a short distance from Abraham Lincoln's home.

PREP 30 minutes **BAKE** 25 minutes

13½ ounces bittersweet chocolate (recommended: 55% cacao), coarsely chopped
1 cup butter
1½ cups bread flour or all-purpose flour
¼ teaspoon baking powder
2 cups sugar
4 eggs
½ teaspoon vanilla

1. Line a 15x10x1-inch baking pan with foil, extending it over the edges of pan. Grease foil. In a medium saucepan, combine the chocolate and butter. Heat and stir constantly over low heat until melted and smooth. Remove from heat. Let the mixture cool for 10 minutes.

2. In a small bowl, stir together flour and baking powder; set aside.

3. In a large mixing bowl, combine sugar, eggs and vanilla. Beat with an electric mixer on medium to high speed for 2 to 3 minutes or until color lightens slightly. Beat or fold in melted chocolate mixture. Add flour mixture to chocolate mixture; stir just until combined. Spread batter evenly into prepared pan.

4. Bake in 350° oven 25 minutes. Cool in pan on wire rack. Use foil to lift uncut brownies out of pan. Cut into bars. **Makes 16 to 32 brownies.**

Per brownie: 385 cal, 22 g fat, 84 mg chol, 106 mg sodium, 47 g carbo, 2 g fiber, 5 g pro.

Lemon Curd Tart

Vanilla bean paste is a terrific convenience product. You get the intense flavor and aroma of a vanilla bean without having to scrape the pod. Look for it at spice and specialty stores.

PREP 25 minutes **COOK** 7 minutes **CHILL** 1 hour **BAKE** 13 minutes **STAND** 40 minutes

4 egg yolks
½ cup sugar
¼ cup freshly squeezed lemon juice
¼ cup unsalted butter or butter, cut up and softened
⅛ teaspoon vanilla bean paste, one 4- to 6-inch vanilla bean or 1 teaspoon vanilla
½ cup whipping cream
Easy Tart Shell (recipe follows)
1 cup blueberries, raspberries, blackberries and/or chopped strawberries

1. In a small nonreactive* heavy saucepan, combine egg yolks and sugar; let stand for 5 minutes. Add the lemon juice; mix well. Cook and stir constantly over medium heat 7 to 8 minutes or until thickened and bubbly and an instant-read thermometer registers 180°.

2. Once lemon curd is very thick, remove from heat and strain through a fine-mesh strainer into a small bowl. Let mixture cool about 20 minutes or until an instant-read thermometer registers 140°. Stir in the butter and, if using, the vanilla paste or vanilla. For vanilla bean, using the tip of a paring knife, slit vanilla bean lengthwise down the center and scrape seeds into the lemon curd.

3. Cover surface of the lemon curd with plastic wrap. Chill at least 1 hour. (Curd can be made up to 1 week ahead and stored, covered, in the refrigerator.)

4. In a chilled metal mixing bowl, beat whipping cream with an electric mixer on medium speed just until soft peaks form. Stir a small amount of the whipped cream into the lemon curd to lighten. Gently but thoroughly fold in the remaining whipped cream.

5. To serve, using a small sharp knife, gently loosen edge of Easy Tart Shell from sides of pan; remove sides of pan. Place tart shell on a serving plate. Spoon the lemon curd mixture into tart shell. Top with berries. Cut tart into wedges. **Makes 8 servings.**

Easy Tart Shell: Let half of a 15-ounce package rolled refrigerated unbaked piecrust (one crust) stand at room temperature 15 minutes; unroll. Ease into an ungreased 11-inch tart pan with a removable bottom. Press pastry into pan and up sides; trim edges. Prick bottom and sides. Line with a double thickness of foil. Bake in a 450° oven for 8 minutes. Remove foil. Bake for 5 to 6 minutes more or until lightly browned. Cool completely in pan on a wire rack.

*Tip: Because acidic foods react to aluminum pans, use a stainless-steel, glass or enamel pan to prepare the curd.

Per serving: 310 cal, 21 g fat, 143 mg chol, 119 mg sodium, 29 g carbo, 0 g fiber, 2 g pro.

Vegan Chocolate-Blueberry Parfait

You don't need to be vegan to appreciate this rich, silky, chocolatey nondairy dessert. Vegans and nonvegans alike love it.

PREP 45 minutes **CHILL** 2 hours **BAKE** 20 minutes **COOL** 10 minutes

1 cup semisweet chocolate pieces
1 12-ounce package silken-style soft tofu (fresh bean curd), drained
⅓ cup maple syrup
2 tablespoons hazelnut liqueur or maple syrup
Chocolate Cake (recipe follows)
1½ cups fresh blueberries, blackberries, raspberries and/or strawberries
3 tablespoons cranberry juice
2 tablespoons maple syrup
1 tablespoon black raspberry liqueur or cranberry juice
Fresh blueberries, blackberries, raspberries and/or strawberries

1. In a double boiler or a heavy small saucepan, cook and stir chocolate over low heat until melted; set aside.

2. In a food processor, combine tofu, ⅓ cup maple syrup and the hazelnut liqueur. Cover and process until mixture is smooth. Add melted chocolate; cover and process until creamy, scraping down sides as needed. Cover; chill 2 to 4 hours.

3. Prepare and cool Chocolate Cake. Cut cake into 1-inch squares. Set aside.

4. In a food processor, combine 1½ cups berries, the cranberry juice, 2 tablespoons maple syrup and the raspberry liqueur. Cover; process until mixture is smooth.

5. Spoon half of the berry puree into the bottom of eight chilled 8- to 10-ounce glasses, such as margarita, martini, parfait or dessert glasses. Top with half of the chilled mousse. Evenly divide the cake pieces among glasses. Top with the remaining mousse and berry puree. Garnish with additional fresh blueberries. Cover and chill any leftovers for up to 24 hours. **Makes 8 servings.**

Chocolate Cake: Grease a 9x9x2-inch baking pan. Line the bottom of pan with waxed paper; grease the paper and flour the pan. Set aside. In a large bowl, combine 2¼ cups all-purpose flour, 1½ cups sugar, ½ cup unsweetened cocoa powder, 1½ teaspoons baking soda and ¾ teaspoon salt. Add 1½ cups hot water, ½ cup olive oil, 1½ teaspoons vanilla and 1½ teaspoons cider vinegar. Beat with an electric mixer on low speed until combined. Beat on medium speed for 1 minute. (Do not overmix.) Spread batter into the prepared pan. Bake in a 375° oven for 20 to 25 minutes or until a wooden toothpick inserted near the center comes out clean. Cool in pan on a wire rack for 10 minutes. Remove from pan; peel off waxed paper. Cool thoroughly on wire rack.

Per serving: 619 cal, 22 g fat, 0 mg chol, 465 mg sodium, 101 g carbo, 5 g fiber, 8 g pro.

Roasted Peach Pies with Butterscotch Sauce

These pies are simply peaches baked in a biscuitlike crust. This recipe makes two 7-inch pies or one 9-inch pie.

PREP 40 minutes   **CHILL** 30 minutes   **BAKE** 33 minutes

    1 cup all-purpose flour
    ½ teaspoon baking powder
    ¼ teaspoon salt
    ¼ cup unsalted butter
    ½ cup sour cream
    1 tablespoon milk
    6 small or 4 medium peaches
      Butterscotch Sauce (recipe follows)
      Vanilla ice cream (optional)
      Fresh mint leaves (optional)
      Freshly ground nutmeg (optional)

1. In a large bowl, combine flour, baking powder and salt. Using a pastry blender or two knives, cut in butter until mixture resembles coarse cornmeal. Stir in sour cream and milk just until combined. Cover and refrigerate 30 minutes or up to 2 days.

2. For two 7-inch pies, divide dough in half. On a lightly floured surface, roll two 8½-inch circles. Transfer to two 7-inch pie plates. (For a 9-inch pie do not divide dough, roll to an 11-inch circle; transfer to a 9-inch pie plate.) Trim crusts even with top of pie plates. With a lightly floured fork, press sides of crust into pie plate. Line with a double thickness of foil coated with nonstick cooking spray. Bake in a 450° oven 8 minutes. Remove foil; bake 5 to 6 minutes more or until crust is golden; cool. Reduce oven to 350°.

3. Cut peaches into thick slices, slicing around the pits. Add peaches to cooled crusts. Cover edges of pies with foil.

4. Bake 20 to 25 minutes or just until peaches are tender. Transfer to a rack. While pies are still warm, drizzle with ¼ cup of the Butterscotch Sauce. Serve immediately (crust becomes soggy as pie sits). Top with ice cream and sprinkle with mint and nutmeg, if you like. Pass remaining Butterscotch Sauce.
Makes 6 to 8 servings.

Butterscotch Sauce: In a small saucepan, melt ¼ cup unsalted butter over medium heat. Stir in ⅓ cup packed brown sugar and 1 tablespoon light-color corn syrup. Bring to a boil and boil gently, uncovered, for 5 minutes, stirring frequently. Stir in 2 tablespoons whipping cream. Cool slightly. Serve immediately. Makes ½ cup.

Per serving: 357 cal, 21 g fat, 56 mg chol, 142 mg sodium, 41 g carbo, 2 g fiber, 4 g pro.

The Horton Bay General Store in Boyne City, Michigan, is home to an antiques store, cafe and B&B. Ernest Hemingway spent time in his youth in Horton Bay and refers to the store—though not by name—in two of his novels.

Peach Ice Cream

Enjoy this ice cream in August at the peak of peach season in Michigan and Missouri.

PREP 5O minutes **CHILL** 4 hours **FREEZE** per manufacturer's directions **STAND** 4 hours to ripen

1 cup sugar
1 cup whipping cream
2⅔ cups half-and-half or light cream
4 egg yolks, lightly beaten
4 teaspoons vanilla
½ teaspoon kosher salt or ¼ teaspoon salt
½ teaspoon freshly grated nutmeg
    or ¼ teaspoon ground nutmeg (optional)
4 cups chopped, pitted and peeled ripe
    peaches or frozen unsweetened peach
    slices, thawed and chopped
1 cup peach nectar or 1 cup evaporated
    milk, chilled
2 tablespoons peach brandy or peach
    liqueur (optional)

1. In a medium heavy saucepan, combine sugar, whipping cream and 1 cup of the half-and-half. Cook over medium-high heat, stirring constantly until mixture just starts to boil. Remove from heat. Whisk about 1 cup of the hot mixture into beaten egg yolks; return all to saucepan. Cook and stir for 1 to 2 minutes or until mixture coats the back of a clean metal spoon. (Do not boil.) Remove from heat. Cool the mixture for 20 minutes.

2. Strain the custard through a fine-mesh sieve into a large bowl. Stir in remaining half-and-half, the vanilla, salt and, if you like, nutmeg. Cover and chill 4 to 24 hours. (It's thicker after chilling.)

3. Place half the peaches in a food processor. Cover and process until pureed and smooth. Stir puree and remaining chopped peaches into chilled custard.

4. Stir chilled peach nectar and, if you like, peach brandy into custard. Transfer mixture to a 4- or 5-quart ice cream freezer. Freeze according to the manufacturer's directions. If you like, ripen* for 4 hours before serving. **Makes 2O (½ cup) servings.**

*Tip: To ripen ice cream in a traditional-style ice cream freezer: After churning, remove the lid and dasher and cover the top of freezer can with waxed paper or foil. Plug the hole in the lid with a small piece of cloth; replace lid on can. Pack the outer freezer bucket with enough ice and kosher or rock salt to cover the top of the freezer can, using 4 cups ice to 1 cup salt.

Nutrition facts per serving: 155 cal, 9 g fat, 65 mg chol, 69 mg sodium, 17 g carbo, O g fiber, 2 g pro.

There are so many ways to enjoy impossibly sweet and juicy summer peaches. Eat them out of hand, in pies and tarts, in crisps and cobblers, and in silky, cooling ice cream. Peach nectar enhances the peach flavor; evaporated milk gives the ice cream a rich texture. You win either way.

PEANUT BUTTER
BUCKEYE BROWNIE
CHEESECAKE, PAGE 177

Fall

French Toast Sticks with Maple-Apple-Nut Topping

Inspired by Breakfast Delights from Corning, Iowa, this recipe uses unfrosted Dutch apple bread from a local bakery. The topping brings similar flavors to the dish.

PREP 25 minutes   **COOK** 4 minutes per slice

4 eggs, lightly beaten
1 cup milk
3 tablespoons sugar
2 teaspoons vanilla
½ teaspoon ground nutmeg or ¾ teaspoon
    ground cinnamon
8 ½- to ¾-inch slices challah bread, brioche,
    crusty whole wheat country-style bread
    or French bread, or 8 slices dry white,
    whole wheat or cinnamon-raisin bread
2 tablespoons butter
    Maple-Apple-Nut Topping (recipe follows)
    Fresh strawberries, raspberries,
      blackberries and/or blueberries
    Powdered sugar
    Whipped cream (optional)

1. In a shallow bowl, beat together eggs, milk, sugar, vanilla and nutmeg. Dip bread slices into egg mixture, letting each side soak about 10 seconds.

2. In a 12-inch skillet or on a griddle, melt 1 tablespoon of the butter over medium heat. Cook half the bread slices 4 to 6 minutes or until golden, turning once. Keep warm in a 200° oven. Repeat with remaining butter and bread.

3. If you like toast sticks, cut the slices of French toast lengthwise into thirds. Serve immediately with Maple-Apple-Nut Topping and strawberries. Sprinkle with powdered sugar. If you like, garnish with whipped cream. **Makes 4 (2 slice) servings.**

Maple-Apple-Nut Topping: In a small saucepan, combine 1 large apple, cored, peeled and chopped; 2 tablespoons water; and ¼ teaspoon ground cinnamon. Bring to boiling over medium heat; reduce heat. Simmer, covered, for 2 to 3 minutes or until apple is just tender, stirring occasionally. Stir in ½ cup maple syrup and ¼ cup chopped toasted almonds, pecans or walnuts. Cook, uncovered, for 2 minutes or until mixture is slightly thickened and heated through.

Per serving: 637 cal, 17 g fat, 236 mg chol, 697 mg sodium, 105 g carbo, 7 g fiber, 20 g pro.

Hearty Multigrain Pancakes

PREP 15 minutes   **COOK** 2 minutes per batch

1 cup all-purpose flour
½ cup whole wheat flour
¼ cup cornmeal
¼ cup quick-cooking rolled oats
2 tablespoons packed brown sugar
2 teaspoons baking powder
¼ teaspoon salt
1½ cups fat-free milk
3 tablespoons canola oil
1 teaspoon vanilla
1 egg
    Warm maple syrup (optional)

1. In a large bowl, stir together the flours, cornmeal, oats, brown sugar, baking powder and salt. In another bowl, beat together the milk, oil, vanilla and egg. Add all at once to flour mixture, stirring just until moistened. (Batter will be lumpy.)

2. For each pancake, pour about ¼ cup batter onto a hot, lightly greased griddle or heavy skillet, spreading the batter if necessary. Cook over medium heat for 1 to 2 minutes on each side or until pancakes are golden brown, turning to the second side when the pancakes have bubbly surfaces and the edges are slightly dry. **Makes 6 (2 pancakes) servings.**

Per serving: 257 cal, 8 g fat, 32 mg chol, 258 mg sodium, 38 g carbo, 2 g fiber, 7 g pro.

Buttermilk Pancakes: Substitute 1¾ cups buttermilk for the milk, reduce baking powder to 1 teaspoon and add ½ teaspoon baking soda.

Multigrain Apple Streusel Muffins

Rise and shine! These tender gems taste so good that you'd never guess the recipe bumps up the fiber with two kinds of whole grains and trades most of the butter for applesauce and buttermilk.

PREP 30 minutes **BAKE** 20 minutes **COOL** 5 minutes

½ cup finely chopped almonds
⅓ cup all-purpose flour
2 tablespoons packed brown sugar
2 tablespoons butter or margarine, melted
1¼ cups all-purpose flour
1 cup spelt flour or whole wheat flour
⅓ cup toasted wheat germ
¼ cup packed brown sugar
1½ teaspoons baking powder
1 teaspoon cinnamon
½ teaspoon baking soda
¼ teaspoon salt
2 eggs, lightly beaten
¾ cup applesauce
¾ cup buttermilk
2 tablespoons butter, melted, or vegetable oil
¾ cup shredded or finely chopped, peeled tender-sweet apple

1. Coat sixteen 2½-inch muffin cups with nonstick spray or line with paper bake cups, and coat paper cups with spray.

2. For topping: In a small bowl, mix almonds, ⅓ cup flour, 2 tablespoons brown sugar and 2 tablespoons melted butter.

3. In a large bowl, mix 1¼ cups all-purpose flour, the spelt flour, wheat germ, ¼ cup brown sugar, the baking powder, cinnamon, baking soda and salt. Make a well in the center.

4. In a small bowl, combine eggs, applesauce, buttermilk and 2 tablespoons melted butter. Add to flour mixture. Stir just until moistened (batter will be lumpy). Fold in apple.

5. Spoon into muffin cups; sprinkle with topping. Bake in 400° oven 20 to 25 minutes or until a toothpick comes out clean. Cool in pan on rack for 5 minutes. Serve warm. **Makes 16 servings.**

Per serving: 161 cal, 6 g fat, 32 mg chol, 155 mg sodium, 23 g carbo, 2 g fiber, 5 g pro.

Midwest orchards offer much more than perfectly at-peak apples. Many peddle slices of warm pie, cider and apple butter, too.

Caramel-Banana Muffins

PREP 30 minutes **BAKE** 18 minutes **COOL** 5 minutes

½ cup chopped pecans
2 tablespoons sugar
1 teaspoon ground cinnamon
1 3-ounce package cream cheese, softened
¼ cup butter, softened
⅔ cup sugar
1 egg
1 medium banana, peeled and mashed
   (½ cup)
1 teaspoon vanilla
1¼ cups all-purpose flour
¾ teaspoon baking powder
¼ teaspoon baking soda
¼ teaspoon salt
2 tablespoons caramel-flavor
   ice cream topping
1 medium banana, peeled and thinly sliced
   (optional)
1 tablespoon butter, melted
   Caramel-flavor ice cream topping
   (optional)

1. Line twelve 2½-inch muffin cups or six jumbo (3¼-inch) muffin cups with paper bake cups. In a small bowl, toss together the pecans, 2 tablespoons sugar and 1 teaspoon cinnamon.

2. In a large mixing bowl, beat the cream cheese, butter and ⅔ cup sugar with an electric mixer on medium speed until well combined. Add the egg and beat well. Beat in the mashed banana and vanilla until mixture is combined.

3. In another bowl, stir together the flour, baking powder, baking soda and salt. Add to the banana mixture, beating on low speed until just combined.

4. Stir in ¼ cup of the pecan mixture. Spoon half the batter into prepared muffin cups (1 rounded tablespoon for each 2½-inch muffin cup or 2 rounded tablespoons for each jumbo muffin cup). Drizzle ½ teaspoon caramel topping over batter in each cup (1 teaspoon for jumbo muffins). Top with remaining batter. If you like, top each muffin with two slices additional banana. Drizzle each with a little melted butter and sprinkle with remaining pecan mixture.

5. Bake the muffins in a 375° oven for 18 to 20 minutes (22 to 24 minutes for jumbo) or until a toothpick inserted in centers comes out clean. Cool in pan on a wire rack for 5 minutes. Remove from pan. Serve warm, drizzled with more caramel topping if you like. **Makes 12 standard or 6 jumbo muffins.**

Per standard muffin: 222 cal, 11 g fat, 38 mg chol, 172 mg sodium, 29 g carbo, 1 g fiber, 3 g pro.

German Chocolate Pecan Rolls

PREP 45 minutes **RISE** 2 hours **BAKE** 25 minutes

2 packages active dry yeast
2½ cups lukewarm water (105° to 115°)
1 teaspoon granulated sugar
1 package (2-layer-size) dark chocolate cake mix
6 cups all-purpose flour
1 egg
⅓ cup vegetable oil
½ teaspoon salt
¼ cup butter, melted
1¼ cups miniature semisweet chocolate pieces
1 cup granulated sugar
1 cup flaked or shredded coconut
⅔ cup butter
1⅓ cups packed brown sugar
⅓ cup light-color corn syrup
2 cups coarsely chopped pecans

1. For dough: In a very large mixing bowl, stir the yeast into ½ cup of the warm water; add the 1 teaspoon sugar. Let mixture stand for 5 minutes or until foamy.

2. Stir the cake mix, 1 cup of the flour, the egg, oil, salt and the remaining water into yeast mixture. Beat with an electric mixer on high speed for 3 minutes, scraping sides of bowl constantly. Using a wooden spoon, stir in the remaining flour to form a soft dough. (Dough will be sticky.) Cover and let rise about 1 hour or until doubled.

3. Lightly grease two 13x9x2-inch baking pans. Set aside. Stir dough down. Cover and let rise again until doubled (about 30 minutes). Stir dough again. Divide in half. Turn one portion of the dough out onto a well-floured surface.* Turn to coat lightly with flour. Roll or pat the dough into a 12x8-inch rectangle. Brush with half of the melted butter.

4. For filling: In a small mixing bowl, mix chocolate pieces, 1 cup sugar and the coconut. Sprinkle half the filling over dough. Roll up into spiral, starting from a long side. Pinch edge to seal.

5. In a saucepan, melt ⅔ cup butter. Stir in 1⅓ cups packed brown sugar and the corn syrup. Cook and stir until sugar melts. Remove from heat. Stir in pecans. Divide pecan mixture between pans.

6. Cut dough spiral crosswise into 12 pieces. Arrange, cut sides down, in a prepared pan. Repeat with the remaining dough, melted butter and filling. Cover loosely; let the dough rise in a warm place until nearly doubled (30 to 45 minutes).

7. Uncover pans. Place a baking sheet under each of the pans. Bake in a 350° oven for 25 to 30 minutes or until lightly brown and rolls sound hollow when lightly tapped. Turn out rolls onto serving platter immediately after baking. Serve warm. **Makes 24 rolls.**

*Note: For easier handling, chill dough 1 hour before rolling or patting out.

Make-ahead directions: Prepare the recipe as directed except do not let rolls rise after shaping. Cover loosely with oiled waxed paper then with plastic wrap. Chill for 2 to 24 hours. Before baking, let rolls stand, covered, for 30 minutes at room temperature. Uncover and bake as directed.

Per roll: 532 cal, 7 g fat, 27 mg chol, 301 mg sodium, 75 g carbo, 3 g fiber, 7 g pro.

Apple Pumpkin Sunflower Bread

A bushel full of fall flavor is packed into this homey loaf: pumpkin, apple, nuts and spices.
A generous half-cup of cider adds unmistakably fruity zing.

PREP 30 minutes **BAKE** 55 minutes **COOL** 10 minutes

1½ cups whole wheat flour
1½ cups all-purpose flour
2¼ teaspoons pumpkin pie spice
2 teaspoons baking soda
1 teaspoon salt
1 cup granulated sugar
1 cup packed brown sugar
1 cup walnut or vegetable oil
4 eggs
½ cup applejack, apple brandy or apple cider
1 15-ounce can pumpkin
1½ cups finely chopped, peeled firm-sweet apple
½ cup dry-roasted sunflower seeds

1. Grease bottom and ½ inch up sides of two 9x5x3-inch, three 8x4x2-inch, or four 7½x3½x2-inch loaf pans. Line bottoms with parchment; grease parchment. In a large bowl, mix flours, pumpkin pie spice, baking soda and salt.

2. In an extra-large mixing bowl, beat sugars and oil with an electric mixer. Add eggs; beat well. Alternately add flour mixture and applejack, beating on low speed after each addition until just combined. Beat in pumpkin. Fold in apple and sunflower seeds. Spread batter into prepared pans.

3. Bake in a 350° oven 55 to 60 minutes for the 9x5-inch loaves, 45 to 50 minutes for the 8x4-inch loaves or 40 to 45 minutes for the 7½x3-inch loaves, or until a toothpick comes out clean.

4. Cool in pans 10 minutes. Remove and cool on racks. Wrap in foil and store overnight before slicing. **Makes 32 servings.**

Per serving: 180 cal, 9 g fat, 23 mg chol, 173 mg sodium, 24 g carbo, 1 g fiber, 3 g pro.

Walnut oil infuses this rich spiced loaf with flavor. Good apple varieties to use in this recipe include Braeburn, Fuji, McIntosh, Jonathan and Newtown Pippin.

PEPPERONI
PIZZA PULL

Pepperoni Pizza Pull

PREP 15 minutes **BAKE** 25 minutes
COOL 5 minutes

- 1 3.5-ounce package sliced pepperoni, chopped
- 1 cup shredded mozzarella cheese (4 ounces)
- ¼ cup grated Parmesan cheese (1 ounce)
- 1 11-ounce package refrigerated breadsticks (12)
- 1 cup pizza sauce, warmed

1. Grease a 9x5x3-inch loaf pan; set aside. In a medium bowl, toss pepperoni, shredded mozzarella and grated Parmesan cheese; set aside.

2. Using kitchen scissors or a sharp knife, cut dough into 1-inch pieces. Arrange one-third of the dough pieces in prepared pan. Top with one-third of the cheese mixture. Repeat layers two more times.

3. Bake, uncovered, in a 350° oven for 25 minutes or until golden brown. Cool in pan for 5 minutes. Remove the loaf from pan. Serve it warm with pizza sauce. **Makes 8 servings.**

Per serving: 231 cal, 11 g fat, 28 mg chol, 699 mg sodium, 23 g carbo, 1 g fiber, 11 g pro.

Thai-Style Butternut Squash Soup

PREP 25 minutes **COOK** 4 to 5 hours (low) or 2 to 2½ hours (high)

- 2 pounds butternut squash, peeled and cut into 1-inch pieces
- 2 cups chicken broth
- 1 14-ounce can unsweetened coconut milk
- ¼ cup finely chopped onion
- 1 tablespoon packed brown sugar
- 1 tablespoon fish sauce or soy sauce
- ½ to 1 teaspoon Asian chili sauce (Sriracha) sauce or crushed red pepper
- 2 tablespoons lime juice

  Thai Gremolata (recipe follows)

  Lime wedges (optional)

1. In a 3½- or 4-quart slow cooker, stir together squash, broth, coconut milk, onion, brown sugar, fish sauce and Asian chili sauce.

2. Cover and cook on low for 4 to 5 hours or on high for 2 to 2½ hours.

3. Use an immersion blender to carefully blend soup until completely smooth. (Or transfer the mixture in batches to a food processor or blender; or use a potato masher to mash mixture nearly smooth.) Stir in lime juice. Ladle into bowls and top with Thai Gremolata. If you like, serve with lime wedges. **Makes 4 to 6 servings**

Thai Gremolata: In a small bowl, stir together ½ cup chopped fresh basil or cilantro, ½ cup chopped peanuts and 1 tablespoon finely shredded lime peel.

Per serving: 189 cal, 10 g fat, 1 mg chol, 581 mg sodium, 24 g carbo, 4 g fiber, 5 g pro.

When the weather turns cool, bread baking and soup making warms the body and soothes the soul. Both of these are perfect recipes for sharing with friends. The pizza bread is a fun, casual appetizer. The soup makes a lovely first course for a more formal dinner.

Stout-Soaked Porterhouse with Beer Butter

Plan on one porterhouse steak to serve two or three people but the marinade will work for up two steaks to serve four to six people.

PREP 35 minutes   **MARINATE** 4 hours   **BROIL** 12 minutes   **STAND** 5 minutes

1 porterhouse steak, 1 inch thick
    (about 1¼ pounds)
1 12-ounce bottle stout beer
1 tablespoon Dijon-style mustard
1 tablespoon Worcestershire sauce
2 teaspoons dried tarragon, crushed
½ teaspoon salt
½ teaspoon ground black pepper
1 shallot, finely chopped
2 teaspoons olive oil
½ cup butter, softened

1. Place steak in a resealable plastic bag set in a shallow dish. Set aside 2 tablespoons beer. In a small bowl, combine remaining beer, the mustard, Worcestershire, 1 teaspoon of the tarragon, the salt and pepper. Pour beer mixture over steak in bag. Marinate in the refrigerator for 4 to 6 hours, turning occasionally.

2. Meanwhile, in a small skillet over medium heat, cook shallot in hot oil 5 minutes or until tender. Stir in reserved 2 tablespoons beer. Remove from heat. Cool 10 minutes. In a small bowl, combine softened butter, shallot mixture and remaining 1 teaspoon tarragon. Transfer mixture to waxed paper; shape into a log. Wrap and freeze.

3. Preheat broiler. Drain steak; reserve marinade. Season steak with additional salt and pepper. Place steak on the unheated rack of a broiler pan. Broil 3 to 4 inches from heat to desired doneness, turning once, 12 to 15 minutes for medium-rare (145°) or 15 to 20 minutes for medium (160°). Transfer to platter. Tent with foil and let stand 5 minutes.

4. Place reserved marinade in a small saucepan. Bring to boiling. Reduce heat to medium and simmer, uncovered, 15 minutes. (Do not overcook; marinade can become bitter.)

5. To serve, slice steak into portions. Drizzle with some of the marinade reduction, and top each with a slice of frozen butter. **Makes 2 to 3 servings.**

Per serving: 502 cal, 25 g fat, 134 mg chol, 1,339 mg sodium, 12 g carbo, 0 g fiber, 41 g pro.

The warm and glowing shades of fall serve as a signal to welcome friends and family to our tables with hearty, comforting foods.

Cranberry-Sausage-Stuffed Pork Chops with Pumpkin Gravy

Watching calories? Half a chop satisfies most people.

PREP 30 minutes **COOK** 14 minutes

4 1½-inch-thick pork chops
   (9 to 10 ounces each)
8 ounces bulk hot pork sausage
½ cup herb stuffing mix
½ cup dried cranberries
½ cup applesauce
1 teaspoon salt
½ teaspoon ground black pepper
2 tablespoons vegetable oil
1 cup fat-free Caesar salad dressing
⅔ cup pumpkin butter
½ cup chicken stock or broth
¼ cup pumpkin seeds (pepitas), toasted

1. Make a pocket in each chop by cutting from fat side almost to bone.

2. In a 4- to 6-quart pressure cooker (or use oven method that follows), crumble pork sausage. Cook and stir until browned; drain in a colander. In a small bowl, combine the pork sausage, stuffing mix, dried cranberries, applesauce, salt and pepper. Spoon one-fourth of the stuffing into each chop. Secure pockets with wooden toothpicks.

3. In cooker, brown chops in hot oil, half at a time, 2 minutes per side. Arrange all in pressure cooker. In a small bowl, whisk together salad dressing, pumpkin butter and chicken stock; pour over chops.

4. Lock lid in place. Place pressure regulator on vent pipe. Over high heat, bring cooker to pressure. Reduce heat just enough to maintain pressure and regulator rocks gently; cook 9 minutes.

5. Quickly release pressure. Carefully remove lid. Transfer chops to platter. Bring liquid in cooker to boil. Reduce heat; simmer, uncovered, 3 to 5 minutes to desired consistency, stirring occasionally.

6. Serve chops topped with pumpkin gravy; sprinkle with pumpkin seeds.
Makes 4 servings.

Oven method: Prepare chops as above, except cook sausage in a large oven-going skillet; brown chops in same skillet. Add salad dressing mixture. Cover; bake in 350° oven 40 minutes. Remove lid. Bake 10 minutes more or until chops are cooked through (145° to 160°). Transfer chops to a serving platter; lightly tent with foil. Carefully return skillet to stove top. Boil gently, uncovered, for 3 to 5 minutes to desired consistency. Serve as above.

Per serving: 1,051 cal, 55 g fat, 237 mg chol, 2,110 mg sodium, 66 g carbo, 3 g fiber, 70 g pro.

Roasted Acorn Squash with Apple-y Sausage

PREP 15 minutes **ROAST** 1 hour 5 minutes

    2 medium acorn squash (1½ to 2 pounds each)
      Olive oil
      Salt
      Freshly ground black pepper
   12 ounces bulk pork sausage
   ½ cup chopped onion (1 medium)
   ½ cup chopped celery (1 stalk)
    1 cup chopped, firm-sweet apples (such
      as Golden Russet, McIntosh, Golden
      Delicious, Honeycrisp, Braeburn, Ginger
      Gold, Pink Lady and/or Cameo; 1 medium)
    1 egg, lightly beaten
   ½ cup sour cream
    1 ounce white cheddar cheese,
      shredded (¼ cup)
    2 tablespoons snipped fresh parsley

1. Cut squash in half lengthwise. Scoop out and discard seeds. Brush inside with olive oil. Sprinkle with salt and black pepper. Arrange squash halves, cut sides down, in a 13x9x2-inch baking pan lined with foil.

2. Roast, uncovered, in a 350° oven for 45 minutes. Remove from oven. Turn squash halves cut side up; set aside.

3. Meanwhile, for filling, in a large skillet, cook sausage, onion and celery over medium-high heat until sausage is brown, using a wooden spoon to break up meat as it cooks. Add apple; cook for 3 minutes more, stirring occasionally. Drain off fat.

4. In a small bowl, combine egg and sour cream. Stir into sausage mixture. Fill squash halves with sausage mixture.

5. Roast, uncovered, in a 350° oven for 20 to 25 minutes more or until squash is tender. Remove from oven. Sprinkle each half with cheese and parsley. **Makes 4 servings.**

Per serving: 545 cal, 35 g fat, 128 mg chol, 793 mg sodium, 44 g carbo, 6 g fiber, 20 g pro.

Pork and Apple Mini Meat Loaves

This moist, sweet and tangy comfort food will remind you of Sunday dinner at Grandma's house. Best of all, it's fast.

PREP 30 minutes **CHILL** 15 minutes **COOK** 15 minutes

   ½ cup bottled chili sauce
    2 tablespoons frozen apple juice
      concentrate, thawed
    2 tablespoons apple butter
   1½ tablespoons apple cider vinegar
    1 teaspoon dry ground mustard
    1 egg
   ¼ cup apple butter
   ½ cup shredded (sweet) apple
    2 teaspoons instant beef bouillon granules
    2 teaspoons dried minced onion
    1 teaspoon minced garlic
   ¼ teaspoon ground pepper
   ⅔ cup quick-cooking oats
    1 pound fresh ground pork
    1 tablespoon vegetable oil
   ½ cup water

1. For glaze: In a small bowl, whisk chili sauce, juice concentrate, 2 tablespoons apple butter, vinegar and dry mustard; set mixture aside.

2. In a large bowl, mix egg, ¼ cup apple butter, shredded apple, bouillon, dried onion, garlic and pepper with oats. Mix in pork. Cover with plastic wrap; refrigerate 15 to 30 minutes.

3. Divide into four portions. Shape each into 4-inch oval loaf. In a large nonstick skillet, brown loaves in hot oil over medium heat, 2 to 3 minutes on each side.

4. Spread 1 tablespoon glaze over each loaf. Pour the water into bottom of skillet. Cover and cook 15 minutes or until loaf centers are cooked through and reach 160°. Pour remaining glaze into the bottom of the skillet. Scrape up brown bits and simmer 1 to 2 minutes more or until glaze is thickened and bubbly. Spoon glaze over mini meat loaves. **Makes 4 servings.**

Per serving: 605 cal, 30 g fat, 128 mg chol, 1,493 mg sodium, 60 g carbo, 3 g fiber, 23 g pro.

It's possible to savor comforting meat loaf even on the busiest weeknights when the loaves are made mini so they cook quickly. Serve with steamed green beans and mashed potatoes.

PORK AND APPLE
MINI MEAT LOAVES

A vineyard along southern Illinois' Shawnee Hills Wine Trail blazes with fall color. The trail runs through several small towns—not a stoplight among them—nestled in the Shawnee National Forest. Visitors stop to sip, shop, hike and admire canopies of brilliant leaves.

Pork Tenderloin with Mushrooms and Onions

This homey supper dish comes from Gunflint Lodge in Grand Marais, Minnesota.

PREP 30 minutes **BAKE** 15 minutes **STAND** 23 minutes

1 pound pork tenderloin
2 eggs, lightly beaten
2 tablespoons water
½ cup fine dry bread crumbs
2 tablespoons olive oil or shortening
4 slices bacon, chopped
2 large onions, halved and thinly sliced
8 ounces sliced fresh mushrooms
½ cup beef, chicken or vegetable broth
½ teaspoon salt
¼ teaspoon dried oregano, crushed
¼ teaspoon ground black pepper

1. Trim fat from meat. Cut meat crosswise into 1-inch slices. In a shallow dish, combine eggs and the water. Place bread crumbs in another shallow dish. Dip meat slices into bread crumbs to coat all sides. Dip into egg mixture. Dip again in bread crumbs to coat all sides. Let slices stand at room temperature for 20 minutes.

2. In a large heavy skillet, cook meat in hot oil over medium-high heat for 3 minutes, turning once halfway. Transfer meat to a 9x9x2-inch baking pan or a 9- to 10-inch metal pie pan. Drain any fat from skillet.

3. In the same skillet, cook bacon until crisp. Using a slotted spoon, remove bacon to paper towels; drain. Add onions to hot pan drippings, stirring to scrape up browned bits. Cook for 8 minutes, stirring occasionally. Add mushrooms; cook and stir for 2 minutes more. Add bacon, broth, salt, oregano and pepper. Bring to boiling; reduce heat. Simmer, uncovered, for 3 minutes or until liquid is reduced by half, stirring to scrape up browned bits. Spoon onion mixture over meat in pan.

4. Bake, uncovered, in a 425° oven about 15 minutes or until meat is slightly pink in center and an instant-read thermometer registers 145°. Remove from oven. Let stand for 3 minutes. **Makes 4 servings.**

Per serving: 374 cal, 17 g fat, 176 mg chol, 797 mg sodium, 19 g carbo, 2 g fiber, 34 g pro.

Mushrooms cooked in a little bacon fat and caramelized sweet onions crown slices of pork tenderloin that are pan-seared and then finished off in the oven.

Chicago-Style Deep-Dish Pizza

PREP 45 minutes **RISE** 1 hour 20 minutes **BAKE** 20 minutes **COOL** 10 minutes

1 package active dry yeast
1 cup warm water (110° to 115°)
3 to 3½ cups all-purpose flour
⅓ cup vegetable oil
½ teaspoon salt
6 ounces bulk mild Italian sausage
12 ounces sliced mozzarella cheese
1 14½-ounce can whole Italian-style
    tomatoes or ½ of a 28-ounce can whole
    Italian-style tomatoes, drained and cut up
1 tablespoon snipped fresh oregano or
    1 teaspoon dried oregano, crushed
1 tablespoon snipped fresh basil or
    1 teaspoon dried basil, crushed
¼ cup grated Parmesan cheese or Romano
    cheese
    Sliced mushrooms or chopped green
    sweet pepper (optional)

1. Generously grease a heavy 10x2-inch round cake pan or 10-inch springform pan with oil; set aside.

2. For crust: In a large mixing bowl, dissolve yeast in the warm water. Let stand 5 minutes. Stir in 1½ cups of flour, ⅓ cup vegetable oil and the salt. Beat with electric mixer on low speed 30 seconds, scraping sides of bowl constantly. Beat for 2 minutes on high speed, scraping the bowl frequently. Using a wooden spoon, stir in as much of the remaining flour as you can. Cover; let rise in a warm place until double (50 to 60 minutes). Punch down. Cover and let rest for 5 minutes.

3. Turn the pizza crust dough into prepared pan. Using oiled hands, press and spread the dough evenly over bottom and 1½ inches up the side of the pan. Cover; let rise in warm place until nearly double (30 to 35 minutes).

4. For meat: In a medium skillet, cook sausage until meat is brown. Drain fat. Pat with paper towels to remove excess fat.

5. To assemble, arrange mozzarella over dough. Spoon meat and tomatoes over cheese. Top with oregano and basil. Sprinkle with Parmesan.

6. Bake in a 500° oven 20 to 25 minutes or until edges of crust are crisp and golden brown and the filling is hot. If you like, sprinkle the pizza with sliced mushrooms or chopped sweet pepper the last few minutes of baking time. If necessary, cover with foil the last 10 minutes of baking to prevent overbrowning. Cool on a wire rack for 10 minutes. If using, remove side of springform pan. Cut into wedges. **Makes 6 to 8 servings.**

Per serving: 666 cal, 38 g fat, 65 mg chol, 969 mg sodium, 55 g carbo, 3 g fiber, 26 g pro.

Brown Ale-Braised Chicken

PREP 25 minutes **STAND** 10 minutes **COOK** 15 minutes **BAKE** 40 minutes

   1 tablespoon packed brown sugar
½ tablespoon chili powder
½ teaspoon salt
¼ teaspoon ground black pepper
¼ teaspoon crushed red pepper
   8 skin-on, bone-in chicken thighs
   1 tablespoon vegetable oil
   1 medium onion, sliced
   2 stalks celery, chopped
   8 small whole carrots with tops, peeled and
      tops trimmed to 1 inch
   2 tablespoons all-purpose flour
   1 12-ounce bottle brown ale
½ cup reduced-sodium chicken broth
   4 cloves garlic, peeled
      Coarsely chopped celery leaves
      Fresh thyme

1. In a small bowl, combine brown sugar, chili powder, salt, ground black pepper and crushed red pepper; rub onto chicken thighs. Let stand 10 minutes.

2. In an extra-large ovenproof skillet, cook chicken in hot oil over medium-high heat until well browned on both sides and skin is crispy. Remove chicken from skillet. Drain fat, reserving 1 tablespoon.

3. In the same skillet, cook and stir the onion, celery and carrots in the reserved fat about 5 minutes or until tender. Stir in flour; cook and stir 1 minute. Stir in beer and broth. Bring to a simmer. Return chicken to skillet. Add garlic. Bake, covered, in a 350° oven for 40 minutes. Sprinkle with celery leaves and thyme.
Makes 4 servings.

Per serving: 552 cal, 34 g fat, 183 mg chol, 571 mg sodium, 23 g carbo, 4 g fiber, 33 g pro.

The rich flavor of beer intensifies during cooking, giving dishes a hearty, perfect-for-fall taste. Like wine, beer can be used as a braising liquid or marinade—as well as making a great addition to a batter or glaze.

Chicken Potpie Soup

PREP 35 minutes BAKE 10 minutes

½ cup chopped carrot
½ cup chopped celery
⅓ cup chopped onion
2 cloves garlic, minced
1 tablespoon butter
½ teaspoon seasoned salt
½ teaspoon dry mustard
½ teaspoon chili powder
½ teaspoon ground black pepper
¼ teaspoon curry powder
4 cups chicken broth
2 cups chopped cooked chicken breast
2 cups dried medium egg noodles
1 cup half-and-half or light cream
1 tablespoon all-purpose flour
1 cup chopped fresh broccoli
⅓ cup frozen peas
   Quick Biscuits (recipe follows)

1. In a saucepan, cook carrot, celery, onion and garlic in hot butter about 5 minutes or until tender. Stir in seasoned salt, mustard, chili powder, black pepper, curry powder, broth, chicken and noodles. Bring to boiling; reduce heat. Simmer, covered, 10 minutes or until noodles are tender. Meanwhile, prepare Quick Biscuits.

2. In a small bowl, whisk together half-and-half and flour; add to saucepan. Add broccoli and peas. Simmer, uncovered, 5 minutes or until slightly thickened. To serve, spoon soup into bowls. Top with Quick Biscuits. **Makes 6 servings.**

Quick Biscuits: In a bowl, combine 2 cups all-purpose flour, 4 teaspoons baking powder, 4 teaspoons sugar and ½ teaspoon cream of tartar. Cut in ½ cup butter to make coarse crumbs. Make a well in center; add ⅔ cup milk. Using a fork, stir just until moistened. On a lightly floured surface, gently knead dough until it holds together. Pat into an 8-inch square. Cut into 12 rectangles; place 1 inch apart on an ungreased baking sheet. Bake in 450° oven for 10 to 12 minutes or until golden.

Per serving: 544 cal, 26 g fat, 117 mg chol, 1,272 mg sodium, 54 g carbo, 3 g fiber, 25 g pro.

Where there's double the carbs, there's double the comfort, right? This homey bowl of chicken soup has chewy egg noodles and a topping of buttery biscuits. You can skip the biscuits, if you like, but then it's just chicken soup (and it's the "potpie" part that makes it special).

Cornish Game Hens with Cider-Sage Sauce

For this easy recipe, just roast the hens on top of the cranberry-apple stuffing in a baking dish. Find Cornish game hens in the supermarket freezer case.

PREP 30 minutes **ROAST** 45 minutes **STAND** 10 minutes

2 1- to 1½-pound fresh or frozen Cornish game hens
2 slices bacon
1 cup coarsely chopped onion (1 large)
1 cup coarsely chopped celery (2 stalks)
1 cup coarsely chopped, unpeeled firm-tart apples
⅔ cup chopped fresh cranberries
1 tablespoon snipped fresh sage leaves
½ teaspoon freshly ground black pepper
¼ to ½ teaspoon ground cinnamon
1 cup dry bread cubes (1½ slices bread)
1 tablespoon water, apple juice or chicken broth
   Olive oil or vegetable oil
   Lemon juice
   Sea salt or kosher salt
   Freshly ground black pepper
   Cider-Sage Sauce (recipe follows)
   Apple slices (optional)
   Lemon wedges (optional)

1. Thaw hens, if frozen. Use kitchen shears or a long, heavy knife to cut hens in half lengthwise. Cut through the breast bone, just off center. If you like, cut on each side of the backbone to completely remove the backbone; discard backbone. If you like, remove and discard as much skin as you can from the hen halves. Set hens aside.

2. For stuffing: In a medium skillet, cook bacon until crisp. Remove bacon and drain on paper towels. Crumble bacon and set aside. Reserve 2 tablespoons of the bacon drippings in skillet. Cook onion and celery in reserved bacon drippings over medium heat until onion is tender. Remove to large bowl. Stir in crumbled bacon, apples, cranberries, sage, ½ teaspoon black pepper and the cinnamon. Stir in bread cubes. Drizzle just enough of the water over bread mixture to moisten, tossing lightly to mix.

3. Spoon the stuffing into four mounds on the bottom of a greased 13x9x2-inch (3-quart) baking dish. Place the hen halves, cut side down, over the stuffing mounds. Brush hens with oil and lemon juice. Sprinkle hens with sea salt and freshly ground black pepper.

4. Roast, uncovered, in a 375° oven for 30 minutes. Meanwhile, prepare the Cider-Sage Sauce.

5. Brush some sauce on the hens, then roast, uncovered, for 15 to 20 minutes more, until hens are tender and no longer pink and an instant-read thermometer registers 170° in breast and 180° in thigh (thermometer should not touch bone), brushing once or twice again.

6. Remove hens from oven. Let stand, loosely covered, for 10 minutes before serving. Transfer hens and stuffing to plates. If you like, garnish dinner plates with sliced apples and lemon wedges. Heat remaining sauce until bubbly and pass at the table. **Makes 4 servings.**

Cider-Sage Sauce: In a small saucepan, stir together 1 tablespoon cornstarch, 1 tablespoon packed brown sugar, ¼ teaspoon ground cinnamon and ¼ teaspoon salt. Stir in 1 cup fresh apple cider or apple juice, 1½ teaspoons snipped fresh sage leaves and 1 clove minced garlic. Cook and stir over medium heat until thickened and bubbly. Cook and stir for 2 minutes more. Remove from heat. Stir in 1 tablespoon applejack, apple brandy or brandy. Makes about 1 cup sauce.

Per serving: 708 cal, 44 g fat, 242 mg chol, 769 mg sodium, 33 g carbo, 3 g fiber, 43 g pro.

Walleye Chowder in Bread Bowls

PREP 15 minutes **COOK** 20 minutes

1 tablespoon butter
1 tablespoon olive oil
2 medium sweet potatoes, peeled and cut
  in ¾-inch cubes (3 cups)
1 cup finely chopped onion
6 cloves garlic, minced
1 28-ounce can crushed fire-roasted
  tomatoes, undrained
1 16-ounce jar salsa
4 ears fresh sweet corn, kernels cut from the
  cob (2 cups)
1 teaspoon salt
1 tablespoon snipped fresh dillweed or
  1 teaspoon dried dillweed
1½ cups whole milk
2 pounds boneless, skinless walleye fillets,
  whitefish or shrimp, cut in 1-inch pieces
1 cup whipping cream
¼ cup chopped fresh cilantro
6 small sourdough bread rounds
4 ounces cheddar cheese, finely shredded
  (1 cup)
⅓ cup sour cream (optional)
  Cilantro (optional)

1. In a Dutch oven, heat butter and oil over medium heat. Add sweet potatoes, onion and garlic. Cook 10 minutes or until nearly tender. Add undrained tomatoes, salsa, corn, salt and dillweed. Bring to boiling; reduce heat. Simmer, uncovered, 5 minutes. Add milk and return to simmer. Add walleye, cream and cilantro; return to simmer. Cook, uncovered, 3 to 5 minutes or until fish flakes when tested with a fork.

2. Slice off top of bread rounds and hollow out center to make a bread bowl. Place bread bowls on baking sheet and place tops, cut side up, alongside bowls. Sprinkle tops with cheese. Bake in a 400° oven 3 to 5 minutes to warm the bowls and melt the cheese.

3. Ladle chowder into bowls. Garnish with sour cream and additional cilantro, if you like. Serve with cheese bread tops. **Makes 6 servings.**

Per serving: 996 cal, 33 g fat, 221 mg chol, 2,246 mg sodium, 119 g carbo, 9 g fiber, 56 g pro.

The fiery, claret-color leaves of a Japanese maple contrast with verdant evergreens and the cool gray of stones along a pond to make a painterly autumn picture.

The number of Midwest wineries has grown exponentially in the past decade. The average monthly production of wine in Iowa alone increased nearly 700 percent from 2002 to 2011.

Penne with Arrabiata Sauce

PREP 30 minutes COOK 20 minutes

  8 ounces packaged dried penne pasta
  1 large onion, chopped
  3 ounces chopped pancetta or ½ cup
     chopped bacon
  4 cloves garlic, minced
  1 tablespoon olive oil
  ½ cup dry red wine or vegetable broth
  1 28-ounce can crushed tomatoes, undrained
  ¼ cup snipped fresh Italian (flat-leaf) parsley
  2 teaspoons dried oregano, crushed
  ½ teaspoon kosher salt or sea salt or
     ¼ teaspoon salt
  ½ to 1 teaspoon crushed red pepper
  ¼ teaspoon freshly ground black pepper
    Snipped fresh Italian (flat-leaf) parsley
    Grated Parmigiano-Reggiano cheese

1. For pasta: In a large saucepan, cook pasta according to package directions. Drain. Return pasta to hot pan; cover and keep warm.

2. For tomato sauce: In a large saucepan, cook onion, pancetta and garlic in hot oil over medium heat for 3 to 4 minutes or until pancetta begins to brown. Remove from heat. Add wine. Return to heat and cook on medium-high heat, scraping up all the brown bits in the pan, for 3 minutes or until almost all the liquid evaporates.

3. Stir in undrained tomatoes, the ¼ cup parsley, the oregano, salt, crushed red pepper and black pepper. Bring to boiling; reduce heat. Simmer, uncovered, for 20 to 30 minutes or until sauce is thickened to desired consistency, stirring occasionally.

4. Toss pasta in hot tomato sauce. Sprinkle each serving with additional snipped parsley and cheese. Serve immediately. **Makes 4 servings.**

Per serving: 420 cal, 11 g fat, 8 mg chol, 638 mg sodium, 63 g carbo, 7 g fiber, 15 g pro.

Lemon-Thyme Roast Chicken with Artichokes

Serve this savory roast chicken with Herbed Brown Rice (page 153). Set aside half the chicken and rice to make Easy Chicken Gumbo (page 153). Use whole roasting chickens rather than broilers or fryers because roasting chickens cook evenly and have better flavor.

PREP 30 minutes   **ROAST** 1 hour 30 minutes   **STAND** 10 minutes

1 4½- to 5-pound whole roasting chicken
2 tablespoons olive oil
2 tablespoons lemon juice
1 teaspoon dried thyme, crushed
½ teaspoon garlic salt
¼ teaspoon freshly ground black pepper
1 16-ounce package peeled fresh baby
   carrots
1 16-ounce package frozen pearl onions
2 tablespoons butter, melted
  Salt
  Ground black pepper
2 6-ounce jars marinated artichoke hearts,
   drained
2 tablespoons all-purpose flour
  Chicken broth or stock
¼ cup milk or half-and-half
4 teaspoons Dijon-style honey mustard
1 teaspoon packed brown sugar
1 teaspoon Worcestershire sauce
  Herbed Brown Rice (page 153)

1. Rinse chicken body and cavity; pat cavity and skin dry with paper towels.

2. To truss the chicken, pull the neck skin over the opening and secure it to the back with a small skewer. Using 100-percent-cotton kitchen string, tie the drumsticks together and fasten to the tail if present. Twist wing tips beneath the chicken (under the back). Place chicken, breast side up, on a rack in a shallow roasting pan. Insert an oven-safe meat thermometer into the center of an inside thigh muscle. Do not let the thermometer touch the bone or the pan.

3. In a small bowl, combine olive oil, lemon juice, thyme, garlic salt and ¼ teaspoon pepper. Brush mixture over the chicken.

4. Arrange carrots and pearl onions around chicken. Drizzle vegetables with butter; season with salt and pepper. Roast in 375° oven, uncovered, for 1 hour. Add drained artichoke hearts. Continue to roast 30 minutes to 1 hour more or until the drumsticks move easily in sockets and chicken is no longer pink (180°).

5. Remove chicken from oven and transfer to a cutting board. Cover loosely with foil; let stand for 10 minutes before carving. Transfer the vegetables to a serving bowl; keep warm. While chicken stands, prepare sauce.

6. For sauce: Pour pan drippings into a large measuring cup. Scrape the browned bits from the pan into the cup. To skim the fat, tip the cup and use a metal spoon to carefully remove the clear fat that rises to the top; reserve fat from the drippings in a separate cup or glass. In a small saucepan, heat 2 tablespoons of the reserved fat (if there is no fat, use 2 tablespoons butter) over medium heat. Stir in flour. Add enough chicken broth to remaining drippings in the measuring cup to equal 1 cup liquid. Add broth mixture and milk to flour mixture in the saucepan. Cook and stir over medium heat until thickened and bubbly. Cook and stir for 1 minute more. Stir in mustard, brown sugar and Worcestershire sauce.

7. Carve the chicken; if you like, reserve half to make Easy Chicken Gumbo (page 153). Store reserved chicken, covered, in the refrigerator for up to 3 days.

8. To serve, spoon the sauce over the remaining carved roast chicken and vegetables. Serve with Herbed Brown Rice (page 153). **Makes 4 servings.**

Per serving: 740 cal, 34 g fat, 104 mg chol, 1,297 mg sodium, 65 g carbo, 6 g fiber, 34 g pro.

EASY CHICKEN
GUMBO

HERBED
BROWN RICE

Easy Chicken Gumbo

Make this weeknight dish with leftover Lemon-Thyme Roast Chicken with Artichokes (page 150) and Herbed Brown Rice (recipe at right). If you like, sprinkle shredded Colby-Monterey Jack cheese over the rice before spooning on the gumbo.

PREP 15 minutes **COOK** 13 minutes

Reserved Lemon-Thyme Roast Chicken
   with Artichokes (page 150)
Nonstick cooking spray
1 9-ounce package frozen cut okra
½ of a 16-ounce package (2 cups) frozen
   (yellow, green and red) sweet pepper
   and onion stir-fry vegetables, chopped
   while frozen
2 14.5-ounce cans reduced-sodium
   chicken broth
1 16-ounce jar chunky salsa
1½ teaspoons Creole seasoning
Reserved Herbed Brown Rice (recipe at
   right)
Baguette-style French bread

1. Chop reserved chicken meat. Set aside.

2. Coat a large saucepan with cooking spray. Add okra and vegetables; cook and stir for 3 minutes over medium-high heat. Add broth, salsa and Creole seasoning. Bring to boiling; reduce heat. Stir in the chicken. Simmer, covered, for 10 minutes.

3. To serve, scoop warm rice into bowls, top each serving with a large spoonful of the gumbo. Serve with French bread. **Makes 6 servings.**

Per serving: 419 cal, 10 g fat, 58 mg chol, 1,647 mg sodium, 53 g carbo, 4 g fiber, 29 g pro.

Herbed Brown Rice

This rice accompanies Lemon-Thyme Roast Chicken with Artichokes (page 150) and Easy Chicken Gumbo (recipe at left).

PREP 10 minutes **COOK** 45 minutes
STAND 5 minutes

2 tablespoons butter
2 cups uncooked brown rice
2 14.5-ounce cans reduced-sodium
   chicken broth
½ cup water
1½ teaspoons dried Italian seasoning
½ teaspoon salt
¼ teaspoon freshly ground black pepper

1. In a large saucepan, melt butter over medium heat. Add rice and cook and stir for 3 minutes. Carefully stir in broth, the water, Italian seasoning, salt and pepper. Bring mixture to boiling; reduce heat. Simmer, covered, for 45 minutes or until rice is tender and liquid is absorbed. Let stand for 5 minutes before transferring to a bowl to serve.

2. If you like, reserve half for Easy Chicken Gumbo (recipe at left). Store, covered, in the refrigerator for up to 3 days. **Makes 12 (½ cup) servings.**

Per serving: 136 cal, 3 g fat, 5 mg chol, 274 mg sodium, 24 g carbo, 1 g fiber, 3 g pro.

Bicyclists take in the fall colors while pedaling the Grand Rounds Scenic Byway. The nation's only urban scenic byway starts in downtown Minneapolis and loops 55 miles around the city, linking lakes, parks and vibrant neighborhoods.

Pimiento Corn Muffins

Serve with Wine-Marinated Pork Roast (recipe at right), and, if you like, save a few to make Corn Muffin Croutons for Thai-Style Salad (recipe page 158).

PREP 20 minutes **BAKE** 18 minutes
COOL 5 minutes

   1 egg, lightly beaten
   1 8.5-ounce package corn muffin mix
   1 cup frozen whole kernel corn
   ⅓ cup milk
   2 tablespoons snipped fresh cilantro
   1 tablespoon diced pimiento
   ½ to 1 teaspoon ground cumin

1. Line eight 2½-inch muffin cups with paper bake cups; set aside.

2. In a medium bowl, combine all ingredients. Stir just until moistened. Spoon ¼ cup batter into each muffin cup.

3. Bake in a 400° oven for 18 minutes or until golden. Cool on a wire rack for 5 minutes. Remove from cups; serve warm, setting aside four in an airtight container for croutons.* **Makes 4 servings.**

*Corn Muffin Croutons: Crumble the reserved muffins into large pieces into a 15x10x1-inch baking pan. Bake in a 400° oven for 8 to 10 minutes or until golden brown and crispy, stirring once.

Per muffin: 153 cal, 4 g fat, 24 mg chol, 225 mg sodium, 26 g carbo, 0 g fiber, 4 g pro.

Wine-Marinated Pork Roast

Serve with mashed potatoes, broccoli and Pimiento Corn Muffins (recipe at left). Use half in Thai-Style Salad (page 158).

PREP 45 minutes **MARINATE** 6 hours **ROAST** 1 hour 45 minutes **STAND** 15 minutes

   1 4- to 5-pound pork loin center rib roast
      (backbone loosened)
   6 cloves garlic, halved lengthwise
   ½ teaspoon fennel seeds
   1¾ cups reduced-sodium chicken broth
   1 cup dry white wine
   1 small onion, thinly sliced and separated
      into rings
   ¼ cup olive oil
   2 large fresh parsley or cilantro sprigs
   2 large fresh marjoram or thyme sprigs
   1 teaspoon celery salt
   1 teaspoon bottled hot pepper sauce
   1 large shallot, finely chopped (¼ cup)
   2 tablespoons all-purpose flour
   1 teaspoon snipped fresh parsley
   1 teaspoon snipped fresh marjoram
      Salt
      Freshly ground black pepper
      Hot mashed potatoes
      Steamed broccoli
      Pimiento Corn Muffins (recipe at left)

1. To prepare roast, insert a small sharp knife into meat to make twelve 1-inch-deep cuts. Push garlic and a few fennel seeds into each slit, using knife tip to carefully hold meat open if needed.

2. For marinade: Place meat in an extra-large resealable plastic bag. In a bowl, combine 1 cup of the broth, the wine, onion, oil, parsley and marjoram sprigs, celery salt and bottled pepper sauce. Pour in bag; seal and turn to coat. Marinate in the refrigerator for 6 to 24 hours, turning occasionally. Drain meat, reserving marinade. Strain marinade through a fine-mesh sieve; discard solids. Store marinade, covered, in the refrigerator.

3. Place meat, rib side down, in a shallow roasting pan. Insert an oven-safe meat thermometer into center. Do not let the thermometer touch the bone or the pan.

4. Roast, uncovered, in a 325° oven for 1¾ to 2¼ hours or until thermometer registers 145° to 150°. Transfer to a cutting board. Cover loosely with foil; let stand for 15 minutes before carving (meat will be 155° to 160° after standing). While meat stands, prepare the sauce and bake Pimiento Corn Muffins (recipe at left).

5. For sauce: Pour 2 tablespoons of the pan drippings into a medium saucepan (discard remaining drippings). Heat over medium heat. Add shallot; cook and stir about 5 minutes or until tender. Stir in flour. Add the remaining ¾ cup chicken broth and ¾ cup of the reserved marinade. Stir over medium heat until thickened and bubbly. Cook and stir for 1 minute more. Add parsley and marjoram. Season to taste with salt and pepper.

6. Carve meat. If you like, reserve half for Thai-Style Salad (page 158), covered, in the refrigerator for up to 3 days. Serve remaining meat with sauce, mashed potatoes, broccoli and warm Pimiento Corn Muffins. **Makes 4 servings.**

Per serving: 681 cal, 31 g fat, 122 mg chol, 1,197 mg sodium, 56 g carbo, 5 g fiber, 40 g pro.

PIMIENTO CORN
MUFFINS

WINE-MARINATED
PORK ROAST

FROZEN FRUIT
CUPS

STACKED BLACK BEAN
ENCHILADA PIE

Stacked Black Bean Enchilada Pie

Leftover Chipotle Black Bean Chili (page 158) fills this easy layered dish. If you like, serve with tossed salad greens and frozen Fresh Fruit Compote (recipe at right).

PREP 15 minutes **BAKE** 40 minutes **STAND** 5 minutes

Reserved Chipotle Black Bean Chili
  (page 158)
1 cup frozen whole kernel corn
1 cup shredded cheddar and Monterey Jack
  cheese blend
6 7- to 8-inch flour tortillas
½ cup salsa verde (tomatillo salsa)
1 avocado, halved, seeded, peeled and
  coarsely chopped
2 tablespoons snipped fresh cilantro
  Sour cream

1. In a medium bowl, combine the chili, the corn and ¾ cup of the cheese.

2. Place a tortilla on the bottom of a lightly greased 2-quart square baking dish. Top with ¾ cup of the chili mixture. Repeat layering with the remaining tortillas and chili mixture. Spread the salsa over the top. Sprinkle with the remaining ¼ cup cheese.

3. Bake, uncovered, in a 350° oven about 40 minutes or until heated through. Let stand for 5 minutes before serving.

4. To serve, cut stack into four wedges. Top with avocado, cilantro and a dollop of sour cream. **Makes 4 servings.**

Per serving: 611 cal, 25 g fat, 33 mg chol, 1,804 mg sodium, 79 g carbo, 11 g fiber, 24 g pro.

The recipes featured on pages 150–158 offer up a two-for-the-money deal: Make Meal 1, stash half, add a few ingredients the next night and—shazam!—you've got Meal 2. Leftovers will never be boring again.

Fresh Fruit Compote

Serve this colorful mix with Chipotle Black Bean Chili (page 158). If you like, use half to make Frozen Fruit Cups (recipe below) to serve with Stacked Black Bean Enchilada Pie (recipe at left).

START TO FINISH 20 minutes

1 teaspoon orange zest
¼ cup orange juice
1 tablespoon finely chopped crystallized
  ginger (optional)
2 cups sliced fresh strawberries
2 cups seedless red or green grapes, halved
1 8-ounce can crushed pineapple (juice
  pack), undrained
1 cup fresh blueberries
1 large banana, cut into bite-size pieces
½ cup finely snipped pitted dates
  Plain Greek yogurt

1. For dressing: In a small bowl, combine orange zest, orange juice, and, if you like, crystallized ginger.

2. For salad: In a large bowl, combine strawberries, grapes, pineapple, blueberries, banana and dates. Toss gently with dressing to evenly coat.

3. If you like, reserve half the compote to make Frozen Fruit Cups (recipe follows).

4. To serve Fresh Fruit Compote, divide remaining fruit mixture among small serving bowls. Top with Greek yogurt. **Makes 4 servings.**

Frozen Fruit Cups: In a medium bowl, combine reserved Fresh Fruit Compote and ½ cup plain Greek yogurt. Spoon mixture into eight 2½-inch muffin cups lined with paper bake cups. Cover and freeze until firm. Let stand at room temperature 20 to 30 minutes before serving. Peel off paper cups to serve.

Per serving: 126 cal, 0 g fat, 0 mg chol, 9 mg sodium, 31 g carbo, 3 g fiber, 3 g pro.

Chipotle Black Bean Chili

If you like, set aside half of this hearty vegetarian chili to use in Stacked Black Bean Enchilada Pie (page 157). Fresh Fruit Compote (page 157) makes a refreshing and healthy side.

PREP 25 minutes **COOK** 25 minutes

3 6-inch yellow corn tortillas, halved
  Vegetable oil
2 fresh yellow banana, poblano or Anaheim
  chile peppers, chopped (see note, page 28)
1 large sweet pepper, any color, chopped
1 large red or yellow onion, chopped
2 to 3 cloves garlic, minced
1 tablespoon olive oil
1 15- to 16-ounce can pinto beans, rinsed
  and drained
1 14- to 15-ounce can black beans, rinsed
  and drained
1 14.5-ounce can diced tomatoes, undrained
1¾ cups water or one 14.5-ounce can
  vegetable broth
1 8-ounce can tomato sauce
¼ cup semisweet chocolate pieces

2 teaspoons chili powder
1½ teaspoons minced canned chipotle
  peppers in adobo sauce
1 teaspoon dried oregano, crushed
¼ to ½ teaspoon salt
  Lime wedges

1. For tortilla strips: Cut tortilla halves crosswise into ½-inch-wide strips. In a large heavy saucepan, heat ½ inch of vegetable oil over medium-high heat. Fry the strips, one-third at a time, for 45 to 60 seconds or until crisp and lightly browned. Using a slotted spoon, remove the strips and drain on paper towels.

2. For chili: In a large saucepan, cook peppers, onion and garlic in hot olive oil over medium heat, stirring occasionally, until vegetables are tender. Stir in remaining ingredients (except lime wedges). Bring to boiling; reduce heat. Simmer, uncovered, for 20 minutes.

3. To make Stacked Black Bean Enchilada Pie (page 157), store half the chili, covered, in the refrigerator for up to 3 days.

4. Serve remaining chili in soup bowls; top with tortilla strips and garnish with lime wedges. **Makes 4 servings.**

Per serving: 260 cal, 11 g fat, 0 mg chol, 713 mg sodium, 36 g carbo, 9 g fiber, 10 g pro.

Thai-Style Salad

Make this light salad with half the Wine-Marinated Pork Roast (page 154) and Corn Muffin Croutons (page 154).

START TO FINISH 30 minutes

  Reserved Wine-Marinated Pork Roast
  (page 154)
⅔ cup bottled regular or light Asian ginger-
  sesame salad dressing
4 cups torn mixed salad greens
1 small cucumber, peeled, halved, seeded
  and thinly sliced
½ cup loosely packed mint leaves
¼ cup thinly sliced green onions
2 tablespoons snipped fresh cilantro
  Corn Muffin Croutons (page 154)

1. Slice reserved meat across the grain into thin, bite-size strips. Place meat strips in a medium bowl.

2. Add dressing to meat strips; toss gently to coat.

3. Divide greens among four dinner plates. Top each with cucumber slices, mint leaves and green onions. Remove meat strips from dressing and arrange over the greens. Drizzle the remaining dressing over all. Sprinkle with snipped cilantro and Corn Muffin Croutons (page 154). **Makes 4 servings.**

Per serving: 618 cal, 34 g fat, 111 mg chol, 775 mg sodium, 40 g carbo, 2 g fiber, 36 g pro.

CORN MUFFIN
CROUTONS,
PAGE 154

THAI-STYLE
SALAD

Apple and Couscous-Bulgur Salad

Studded with dried cherries and almonds, this hearty salad pairs well with roast pork or even barbecue. Fresh lemon juice add a touch of pucker that keeps the salad from tasting too sweet.

PREP 15 minutes **COOK** 10 minutes **CHILL** 2 hours

- 2 cups water
- ½ cup bulgur
- ¾ teaspoon sea salt or kosher salt
- ½ teaspoon ground cumin
- ½ cup couscous
- ⅓ cup olive oil
- 1 teaspoon lemon zest
- ¼ cup lemon juice
- 1 tablespoon honey
- 1 tablespoon fresh apple cider
- ¼ teaspoon sea salt or kosher salt
- ¼ teaspoon black pepper
- 1 cup coarsely chopped or torn radicchio or coarsely shredded red cabbage
- ½ cup dried tart red cherries
- 1 cup thinly sliced, unpeeled tender-tart apple
- 1 cup coarsely chopped, unpeeled tender-sweet apple
- 6 large cabbage leaves or lettuce cups
- 2 tablespoons sliced almonds, toasted

1. In a saucepan, bring the water, bulgur, ¾ teaspoon sea salt and cumin to boiling. Reduce heat and cover. Simmer 10 minutes or until bulgur is nearly tender. Remove from heat. Stir in couscous. Cover; let stand 5 minutes, then fluff. Transfer to bowl; let cool slightly.

2. For vinaigrette: In a bowl, whisk together oil, lemon zest, lemon juice, honey, cider, ¼ teaspoon sea salt and the pepper.

3. Drizzle vinaigrette over grains; toss to coat. Stir in radicchio and cherries. Cover and chill for at least 2 and up to 8 hours.

4. Just before serving, stir the apples into couscous mixture. Spoon salad into cabbage leaves. Sprinkle with almonds. **Makes 6 servings.**

Per serving: 292 cal, 13 g fat, 0 mg chol, 339 mg sodium, 42 g carbo, 5 g fiber, 5 g pro

Tuscan Cheese Potato Bake

PREP 30 minutes **BAKE** 20 minutes

- 2 pounds red potatoes
- 3 or 4 cloves garlic, minced
- 1½ teaspoons snipped fresh thyme or ½ teaspoon dried thyme, crushed
- ¼ cup butter
- 1 cup buttermilk
- ½ teaspoon salt
- ¼ teaspoon black pepper
- 1 cup shredded fontina cheese (4 ounces)
- 1 cup finely shredded Parmesan cheese (4 ounces)
- ⅓ cup crumbled blue cheese
- ½ cup panko (Japanese-style bread crumbs)
- ¼ teaspoon dried Italian seasoning, crushed
- 1 tablespoon olive oil
  Snipped fresh parsley (optional)

1. Lightly grease a 2-quart square baking dish; set aside. Scrub potatoes; cut in 1-inch pieces. In large saucepan, cook potatoes in lightly salted boiling water 12 to 15 minutes or until tender; drain.

2. In a 12-inch skillet, cook and stir garlic and thyme in butter over medium heat for 1 minute; add potatoes. Coarsely mash potatoes. Stir in buttermilk, salt and black pepper. Fold in fontina cheese, half of the Parmesan and all the blue cheese. Evenly spread in prepared baking dish.

3. In a small bowl, combine remaining Parmesan, panko, Italian seasoning and oil; toss with a fork to combine. Evenly sprinkle over potato mixture in dish. Bake in a 400° oven for 20 minutes or until bubbly and top is golden. If you like, sprinkle with snipped fresh parsley. **Makes 8 to 10 servings.**

Per serving: 304 cal, 18 g fat, 47 mg chol, 653 mg sodium, 23 g carbo, 2 g fiber, 14 g pro.

TUSCAN CHEESE
POTATO BAKE

Fall is the best time to let
a cool breeze carry you
somewhere new. How about
a tour that takes you on
a 1,200-mile loop around
Lake Superior and through
parts of Michigan, Wisconsin,
Minnesota and Ontario?
Along the way, hit spots that
are by turns arty, woodsy,
upscale and spectacular.

Nutty Caramel Apple Crisp

A double dose of caramel—baked in with the fruit and drizzled on top—elevates the humble crisp to new levels of indulgence. Two varieties of apple ensure the harvest flavor sings.

PREP 45 minutes   **BAKE** 35 minutes
COOL 15 minutes

½ cup all-purpose flour or whole wheat flour
⅓ cup regular rolled oats
½ cup packed brown sugar
1 teaspoon apple pie spice
6 tablespoons butter
⅔ cup coarsely chopped pecans or walnuts
½ cup granulated sugar
¼ cup all-purpose flour
1 teaspoon apple pie spice
3 cups thinly sliced, peeled tender-tart apples
3 cups thinly sliced, peeled firm-sweet apples
2 tablespoons milk
¾ cup caramel ice cream topping
    Vanilla ice cream

1. For topping: Stir together first four ingredients. Cut in the butter until mixture resembles coarse crumbs. Stir in pecans.

2. For filling: In a large bowl, stir together the ½ cup granulated sugar, the ¼ cup flour and the 1 teaspoon apple pie spice. Add the apples and gently toss until coated. Transfer to a 9x9x2-inch (2-quart) square baking dish. Press fruit gently to make an even, slightly mounded surface.

3. In a small bowl, whisk the milk into 2 tablespoons of the caramel topping. Drizzle over apples. Sprinkle with topping. Set the dish on a foil-lined baking sheet.

4. Bake, uncovered, in a 375° oven for 35 to 40 minutes or until apples are tender. Cool for 15 to 20 minutes on a wire rack.

5. Warm the remaining caramel topping and drizzle over crisp. Serve with ice cream.
Makes 8 servings.

Per serving: 640 cal, 29 g fat, 65 mg chol, 204 mg sodium, 89 g carbo, 5 g fiber, 7 g pro.

Michigan is one of the top six apple-producing states. In fact, its state flower is the apple blossom. The profuse and fragrant spring blossoms turn into crisp, fresh apples in the fall.

Paradise Pumpkin Pie

PREP 40 minutes **CHILL** 30 minutes **BAKE** 1 hour

1 8-ounce package cream cheese, softened
¼ cup granulated sugar
½ teaspoon vanilla
1 egg, lightly beaten
  Pastry for Single-Crust Pie (recipe follows)
1¼ cups canned pumpkin
1 cup evaporated milk
2 eggs, lightly beaten
¼ cup granulated sugar
¼ cup packed brown sugar
1 teaspoon ground cinnamon
¼ teaspoon salt
¼ teaspoon ground nutmeg
½ cup chopped pecans
2 tablespoons butter, softened
2 tablespoons all-purpose flour
2 tablespoons packed brown sugar

1. In a small bowl, beat cream cheese, ¼ cup granulated sugar, the vanilla and one egg with an electric mixer until mixture is smooth. Chill the cream cheese mixture in the refrigerator for 30 minutes.

2. Meanwhile, prepare Pastry for Single-Crust Pie. On a lightly floured surface, use hands to slightly flatten the pastry. Roll pastry from center to edge to form a 12-inch circle. Transfer pastry to a 9-inch pie plate; ease into the pie plate, being careful not to stretch pastry. Spoon cream cheese mixture into pastry-lined pie plate. Trim pastry to ½ inch beyond edge of plate. Fold under the extra pastry. Crimp edge as you like.

3. In a medium bowl, stir together pumpkin, evaporated milk, the two eggs, the ¼ cup granulated sugar, ¼ cup brown sugar, the cinnamon, salt and nutmeg. Carefully pour pumpkin mixture over cream cheese mixture.

4. Cover the edge of the pie with foil. Bake in a 350° oven for 25 minutes. Remove the foil; bake for 25 minutes more. Meanwhile, toss together the pecans, butter, flour and the 2 tablespoons brown sugar. Sprinkle over the partially baked pie. Return pie to oven and bake for 10 to 15 minutes more or until a knife inserted near the center comes out clean. Cool pie on wire rack. Store in the refrigerator. **Makes 8 servings.**

Pastry for Single-Crust Pie: In a mixing bowl, stir together 1¼ cups all-purpose flour and ¼ teaspoon salt. Using a pastry blender, cut in ⅓ cup shortening until the pieces are pea size. Sprinkle 1 tablespoon of cold water over part of the mixture; gently toss mixture with a fork. Repeat moistening the dough, using 1 tablespoon cold water at a time, until all of the dough is moistened (4 to 5 tablespoons cold water total). Form the dough into a ball.

Per serving: 493 cal, 30 g fat, 127 mg chol, 323 mg sodium, 48 g carbo, 3 g fiber, 10 g pro.

Bright and beautiful pumpkins—whether solid in color or striated, rotund or slender, round or oblong—announce in no uncertain terms that fall has arrived.

Brown Butter Tarts with Sour Cherries

Browned butter—called beurre noisette *in French for its hazelnut color and flavor—has a distinctive, nutty taste. It adds a special touch to baked goods.*

PREP 40 minutes **CHILL** 2 hours **BAKE** 25 minutes **COOL** 1 hour

Tart Dough (recipe follows)
½ cup butter
2 eggs
½ cup sugar
½ cup cake or pastry flour
½ cup snipped dried tart red cherries, dried figs or pitted whole dates
Cardamom Whip (recipe follows)

1. Prepare Tart Dough. On lightly floured surface, roll chilled Tart Dough from center to edges to form a 13- to 14-inch circle, about ⅛ inch thick. Cut six 4½-inch rounds from the dough. Press rounds firmly into bottom and up sides of six 4-inch individual tart pans with removable bottoms. If necessary, reroll scraps for final crust. Trim crusts even with top of pans. Cover; chill 2 hours.

2. In a small heavy saucepan, cook butter over low to medium heat about 15 minutes or until it turns the color of light brown sugar. (Butter should smell nutty, but not burnt. Brown/black specks are normal.) Set aside to cool slightly, but keep butter in liquid form.

3. In a large mixing bowl, beat eggs and sugar with whip attachment on an electric mixer on medium to high speed for 4 to 5 minutes or until triple in volume and light lemon color. Using a rubber spatula, fold browned butter into egg mixture. Sift flour over butter mixture and fold to combine.

4. Pour into pastry-lined tart pans. Top each with dried fruit. Place tart pans in a 15x10x1-inch baking pan. Bake in a 350° oven for 25 to 28 minutes or until tarts are golden and filling springs back slightly when touched. Cool in pans on wire rack 1 hour. To serve, remove sides from tart pans. Serve warm with Cardamom Whip. **Makes 6 servings.**

Tart Dough: In a large mixing bowl of an electric stand mixer with a paddle attachment, combine one 3-ounce package cold cream cheese, cut into small pieces, and ½ cup cold butter, cut into small pieces. Beat on medium speed for 30 seconds. Add ¾ cup cake flour. Beat on medium speed just until combined (dough should be slightly lumpy). Gather and pat dough into 6-inch circle. Wrap with plastic wrap; chill 2 to 24 hours. Makes enough dough for six 4-inch tart shells.

Cardamom Whip: Using the tip of a paring knife, slit one 4- to 6-inch vanilla bean lengthwise. Using side of knife, scrape seeds from half of vanilla bean; set aside. Wrap remaining half of bean with plastic wrap and reserve for another use. In a chilled mixing bowl, combine 1 cup whipping cream, 1 tablespoon powdered sugar (optional), the vanilla seeds or ½ teaspoon vanilla, ½ teaspoon orange zest, and ¼ teaspoon ground cardamom, cinnamon or nutmeg. Beat with chilled beaters of electric mixer on medium speed until soft peaks form. Makes about 2 cups.

Per serving: 1,070 cal, 53 g fat, 222 mg chol, 310 mg sodium, 133 g carbo, 3 g fiber, 15 g pro.

If ever a fussy dessert was worth the fuss, this is it. Cream-cheese tart dough cradles a brown-butter filling studded with dried tart cherries that is topped with cardamom-and-vanilla flavored whipped cream. Need we say more?

Spiked Apple and Pecan Tart

PREP 45 minutes **FREEZE** 45 minutes **CHILL** 30 minutes **BAKE** 12 minutes **COOK** 10 minutes

⅓ cup butter, cut into small pieces
¾ cup pecans, toasted
¼ cup packed light brown sugar
1¼ cups all-purpose flour
½ teaspoon salt
2 egg yolks
2 tablespoons ice water
3 tablespoons butter
¼ cup granulated sugar
¼ cup applejack, apple brandy or dry sherry
2 tablespoons lemon juice
5 unpeeled firm-tart apples, cored and cut into ¼-inch-thick rings
⅓ cup apple jelly
2 tablespoons applejack, apple brandy or dry sherry
½ cup coarsely chopped pecans, toasted
Sweetened whipped cream

1. Freeze the ⅓ cup chopped butter for at least 30 minutes. In a food processor, combine the ¾ cup pecans and the brown sugar until nuts are finely chopped. Add flour and salt; combine with about 10 on/off pulses. Add frozen butter; process with about 30 pulses until pieces are pea size or smaller. Add egg yolks and the ice water; process with about 10 pulses, until the pastry just comes together but is crumbly with visible bits of butter.

2. Transfer to a bowl and gently knead just until a ball forms. Pat into a 6-inch disk. Wrap in plastic wrap and chill for 30 to 60 minutes, until easy to handle.

3. Lightly butter an 11-inch tart pan with a removable bottom. On a lightly floured surface, roll pastry into a 13-inch circle. Wrap pastry around the rolling pin and unroll it into the tart pan, pressing any spots that tear to seal. Press pastry into fluted sides of tart pan; trim edges. Use a fork to prick the bottom and sides of the pastry shell; be sure to prick where bottom and sides meet. Place on a baking sheet and freeze for 15 minutes.

4. Bake in a 425° oven about 12 minutes or until golden. Cool on a wire rack.

5. In a 12-inch nonstick skillet, melt the 3 tablespoons butter over medium heat. Stir in granulated sugar, the ¼ cup applejack and the lemon juice. Add apple slices to the hot butter mixture. Bring to boiling; reduce heat. Simmer, uncovered, about 8 minutes or until apples are tender and most of the liquid is evaporated, gently rearranging apples and occasionally spooning butter mixture over apples. As slices become tender, transfer with tongs or slotted spoon to the pastry shell, overlapping slices slightly. Gently boil remaining liquid until thick. Pour evenly over the apples.

6. In the same skillet, combine apple jelly and the 2 tablespoons applejack; melt jelly over low heat. Brush mixture over apples. Sprinkle with the ½ cup pecans.

7. To serve, remove sides from tart pan. Serve warm or at room temperature with sweetened whipped cream. Cover and chill within 2 hours. **Makes 8 servings.**

Per serving: 531 cal, 30 g fat, 98 mg chol, 267 mg sodium, 58 g carbo, 5 g fiber, 5 g pro.

Cafe Latté's Turtle Cake

Staff at Cafe Latté in Saint Paul, Minnesota, created their famous Turtle Cake in 1985. It's still a star. Thick caramel topping works best in this recipe. Some of the caramel will ooze from the cake as it chills.

PREP 40 minutes **BAKE** 22 minutes **COOL** 10 minutes **CHILL** 1 hour

Unsweetened cocoa powder
1 egg, lightly beaten
1 cup buttermilk or sour milk*
⅔ cup vegetable oil
2 cups all-purpose flour
1¾ cups sugar
½ cup unsweetened cocoa powder
1 tablespoon baking soda
1 teaspoon salt
1 cup freshly brewed hot coffee
Chocolate Frosting (recipe follows)
1½ cups pecan halves, toasted
½ cup purchased caramel ice cream topping

1. Grease three 9-inch cake pans.** Line the bottom of each cake pan with parchment paper. Grease the paper; dust with unsweetened cocoa powder. Set the prepared pans aside.

2. In a small bowl, stir together egg, buttermilk and vegetable oil; set aside. In a large mixing bowl, stir together flour, sugar, ½ cup cocoa powder, baking soda and salt. Gradually add the buttermilk mixture to flour mixture, beating with an electric mixer until combined. Gradually beat in hot coffee. Pour batter into prepared pans. (Layers will appear shallow.)

3. Bake in a 350° oven for 22 to 25 minutes or until a wooden toothpick inserted near center comes out clean. Cool cakes in pans on wire racks for 10 minutes. Loosen sides from pans, then invert cake layers on racks. Remove the cake layers from pans. Peel off paper; cool thoroughly.

4. When the cake layers are cool, make the Chocolate Frosting. Place one cake layer, top side down, onto a serving plate with a lip (to catch excess icing). Using an icing spatula or wide knife, work quickly to frost the top of this layer with one-third of the frosting. Arrange one-third of the pecans on top and drizzle with some of the ice cream topping. Top with the second layer, top side down. Repeat with frosting, pecans and caramel topping. Top with the third layer, top side up. Repeat with remaining frosting, pecans and caramel topping. Chill cake 1 to 2 hours before serving. **Makes 12 to 16 servings.**

Chocolate Frosting: In a medium saucepan, stir together 1 cup sugar and ½ cup milk. Add 6 tablespoons butter, cut up. Bring the mixture to boiling, stirring constantly. Remove from heat. Add one 12-ounce package semisweet chocolate pieces (2 cups). Using a wire whisk, mix in the chocolate until smooth. If the frosting is too thick or grainy, stir in 1 to 2 teaspoons of freshly brewed hot coffee. If necessary, let stand several minutes before using. Makes about 2½ cups of frosting, enough for this cake.

*How to make sour milk: Don't have buttermilk? Substitute sour milk. For a cup of sour milk, place 1 tablespoon lemon juice or vinegar in a glass measuring cup. Add enough milk to make 1 cup total liquid; stir. Let mixture stand 5 minutes before using.

**Note: If you only have two 9-inch cake pans, refrigerate one-third of the cake batter while you bake the two. Clean and prepare one of the pans as directed, and bake the last layer.

Per serving: 697 cal, 36 g fat, 35 mg chol, 629 mg sodium, 94 g carbo, 4 g fiber, 8 g pro.

Spiced Sweet Potato Cake

PREP 45 minutes BAKE 55 minutes COOL 2 hours

Nonstick spray for baking
2¼ cups all-purpose flour
1½ teaspoons baking powder
1½ teaspoons baking soda
2 teaspoons ground cinnamon
1 teaspoon ground ginger
¼ teaspoon ground cloves
1 teaspoon salt
1 29-ounce can cut sweet potatoes in syrup
1⅔ cups granulated sugar
1 teaspoon imitation maple flavor
1 cup vegetable oil
3 eggs
1⅓ cups spiced pecans, coarsely chopped
3 ounces cream cheese, softened
1 cup whipping cream
3 tablespoons powdered sugar
1 tablespoon pure maple syrup
1 teaspoon imitation maple flavor

1. Coat 10-inch fluted tube pan with nonstick spray. In a large bowl, combine flour, baking powder, soda, cinnamon, ginger, cloves and salt. Drain sweet potatoes, reserving 2 tablespoons liquid. Process potatoes and reserved liquid in food processor until smooth, scraping sides as needed.

2. In a large bowl, beat potato puree, sugar, 1 teaspoon maple flavor and oil with electric mixer until smooth. Add eggs, one at a time, beating after each. Gradually beat in flour mixture. Stir in pecans.

3. Pour into pan. Bake in 350° oven 55 to 60 minutes or until toothpick inserted in cake comes out clean. Lay foil over top of pan the last 10 minutes to prevent overbrowning. Cool in pan 10 minutes; invert onto cooling rack. Remove pan; cool 2 hours.

4. In a large bowl, beat cream cheese with mixer to lighten. Add cream, powdered sugar, maple syrup and 1 teaspoon maple flavor; beat until stiff peaks form. Dust cake with additional powdered sugar. Top with whipped cream cheese. Sprinkle with additional cinnamon.
Makes 10 to 12 servings.

Per serving: 774 cal, 43 g fat, 98 mg chol, 576 mg sodium, 93 g carbo, 4 g fiber, 8 g pro.

Chocolate Oatmeal Cake

Wild rice adds chewiness to this moist cake from Salty Tart in Minneapolis.

PREP 20 minutes BAKE 35 minutes

1 cup quick-cooking rolled oats
½ cup cooked wild rice
½ cup butter, cut up and softened
1½ cups boiling water
1 cup granulated sugar
1 cup packed brown sugar
2 eggs
1 cup all-purpose flour
2 tablespoons unsweetened cocoa powder
1 teaspoon baking soda
½ teaspoon salt
1 cup semisweet chocolate pieces or milk chocolate pieces
2 tablespoons powdered sugar (optional)
2 teaspoons unsweetened cocoa powder (optional)

1. In a large bowl, combine oats, rice and butter. Pour the boiling water over the oat mixture and let stand 10 minutes. Grease and flour a 13x9x2-inch baking pan.

2. Add the sugars to oat mixture; stir until butter melts. Stir in eggs. Add flour, 2 tablespoons cocoa powder, the soda and salt; stir until combined. Stir in ½ cup of the chocolate pieces. Pour into pan. Sprinkle with remaining chocolate pieces.

3. Bake in a 350° oven 35 to 40 minutes or until a wooden toothpick inserted near the center of cake comes out clean. Cool completely in pan on a wire rack. Dust with powdered sugar and 2 teaspoons cocoa powder, if you like. **Makes 20 servings.**

Per serving: 213 cal, 8 g fat, 33 mg chol, 166 mg sodium, 35 g carbo, 1 g fiber, 3 g pro.

CHOCOLATE
OATMEAL CAKE

OPAL'S WALNUT
SHORTBREAD
COOKIES

Opal's Walnut Shortbread Cookies

Patrick Groth, owner-chef of Incredibly Delicious in Springfield, Illinois, uses his grandmother's recipe for these cookies.

PREP 25 minutes **BAKE** 13 minutes per batch

½ cup unsalted butter, softened
⅔ cup sugar
¾ teaspoon salt
1 egg
2 teaspoons vanilla
2 cups all-purpose flour
1½ cups chopped walnuts
   Powdered Sugar Icing (recipe follows; optional)

1. In a large mixing bowl, beat butter for 30 seconds. Add sugar and salt. Beat until combined, scraping sides of bowl occasionally. Beat in egg and vanilla until combined. Beat in as much of the flour as you can with the mixer. Stir in any remaining flour. Stir in walnuts.

2. Drop dough by rounded teaspoons 2 inches apart onto ungreased cookie sheets. Using your fingers, flatten dough.

3. Bake in a 325° oven for 8 minutes. Rotate cookie sheet front to back. Bake for 5 minutes more or until edges are firm and tops are lightly browned. Transfer cookies to a wire rack; cool completely. If you like, drizzle cookies with Powdered Sugar Icing. **Makes 30 cookies.**

Powdered Sugar Icing: In a small bowl, stir together 1 cup powdered sugar, 1 tablespoon milk and ¼ teaspoon vanilla. Stir in additional milk, 1 teaspoon at a time, to make a drizzling consistency. If you like, tint with a few drops of food coloring.

Per cookie: 116 cal, 7 g fat, 15 mg chol, 61 mg sodium, 12 g carbo, 1 g fiber, 2 g pro.

Peanut Butter Buckeye Brownie Cheesecake

Buckeye candy from Ohio was the muse for this outrageously rich and creamy dessert. (Pictured on page 114.)

PREP 45 minutes **BAKE** 28 minutes **CHILL** 4 hours

1 19½-ounce package brownie mix
¾ cup hot fudge-flavor ice cream topping, warmed
2 8-ounce packages cream cheese, softened
1½ cups crunchy peanut butter
1 14-ounce can sweetened condensed milk
1½ cups whipping cream
2 tablespoons powdered sugar
4 chocolate-covered peanut butter cups, chopped
2 tablespoons chocolate-flavor syrup

1. Prepare brownie mix according to package directions, using the 13x9x2-inch pan option. Cool in pan on a wire rack. Cut into bars. Press three-fourths of the brownies into the bottom of a 9-inch springform pan to form a crust. Spread with fudge topping; set aside. Crumble remaining brownies; set aside.

2. In a large mixing bowl, beat cream cheese and peanut butter with an electric mixer on medium speed until just combined. Add sweetened condensed milk; beat until just combined. In a medium bowl, beat whipping cream until soft peaks form. Add powdered sugar; beat until stiff peaks form. Reserve ½ cup of the whipped cream mixture. Fold remaining whipped cream into cream cheese mixture.

3. Spread half of the cream cheese mixture over the hot fudge topping. Sprinkle with one-half of the reserved brownie crumbles. Spread remaining cream cheese mixture over the brownies. Top with the reserved ½ cup whipping cream mixture. Sprinkle remaining brownie crumbles and chopped peanut butter cups over the top. Drizzle with chocolate syrup. Cover and chill the dessert for 4 to 24 hours. **Makes 20 servings.**

Per serving: 552 cal, 37 g fat, 77 mg chol, 306 mg sodium, 50 g carbo, 2 g fiber, 10 g pro.

Mocha Napoleons

Puff pastry is traditionally used in this recipe. An easy-to-make piecrust pastry simplifies this dessert.

PREP 20 minutes **BAKE** 13 minutes **COOL** 20 minutes **CHILL** 15 minutes

  Chocolate Pastry (recipe follows)
1 tablespoon granulated sugar
1 8-ounce carton mascarpone cheese
¼ to ⅓ cup powdered sugar
1½ teaspoons vanilla
  Dash salt
1 teaspoon instant espresso coffee powder
  or instant coffee crystals
½ cup whipping cream
1 tablespoon powdered sugar
1 teaspoon unsweetened cocoa powder

1. Prepare pastry. Divide into three portions. On a lightly floured surface, roll each portion into a 12x4-inch rectangle; if necessary, trim edges until even. Place on baking sheets. Sprinkle granulated sugar evenly over tops of pastry. Bake in a 400° oven for 13 to 15 minutes or until crisp. Transfer to a wire rack; cool.

2. In a large bowl, combine mascarpone, the ¼ to ⅓ cup powdered sugar, vanilla and salt until smooth. In a chilled metal mixing bowl, dissolve espresso powder in whipping cream and beat with electric mixer until soft peaks form. Gently fold whipped cream into mascarpone mixture. Cover; chill for at least 15 minutes.

3. To assemble, spoon half of the filling evenly on one of the pastry rectangles. Top with another pastry rectangle. Spoon remaining filling evenly on pastry stack. Top with remaining pastry.

4. In a small bowl, mix the 1 tablespoon powdered sugar with the cocoa powder. Sprinkle top of pastry stack with powdered sugar mixture. Serve immediately or chill for up to 4 hours before serving.
Makes 8 to 10 servings.

Chocolate Pastry: In a medium bowl, stir together 1⅓ cups all-purpose flour, 2 tablespoons unsweetened cocoa powder, 2 tablespoons sugar and ½ teaspoon salt. Using a pastry blender, cut in ¼ cup shortening and ¼ cup butter (cut up) until pieces are pea size. Using ¼ to ⅓ cup ice water, sprinkle 1 tablespoon at a time over part of the flour mixture; toss with a fork. Push moistened pastry to side of bowl. Repeat, using 1 tablespoon water at a time, until all the flour mixture is moistened. Shape into a ball; knead gently until it holds together.

Per serving: 400 cal, 31 g fat, 72 mg chol, 227 mg sodium, 28 g carbo, 1 g fiber, 9 g pro.

A bench offers respite and a romantic view of the fall color in the 280,000-acre Shawnee National Forest in southern Illinois.

VIENNA ALMOND
CUTOUTS, PAGE 226

Winter

Gingerbread Waffles with Hot Lemon Curd Sauce

A dollop of silky lemon curd sauce gives these spicy waffles a sweet-tart touch. Be careful not to overcook them.

PREP 25 minutes **COOK** per manufacturer's directions

  2 cups all-purpose flour
  1 teaspoon ground cinnamon
1½ teaspoons baking soda
1½ teaspoons ground ginger
  ½ teaspoon ground cloves
  ½ teaspoon salt
  3 egg yolks, lightly beaten
  1 cup molasses
  ½ cup buttermilk
  ½ cup butter, melted
  2 egg whites
    Hot Lemon Curd Sauce (recipe follows; optional)
    Powdered sugar (optional)

1. In a large bowl, combine flour, cinnamon, baking soda, ginger, cloves and salt; make a well in the center and set aside. In a small bowl, combine egg yolks, molasses, buttermilk and butter. Add to flour mixture. Stir just until moistened (batter will be lumpy). Set aside.

2. In a small bowl, beat egg whites with an electric mixer on medium speed for 1 to 1½ minutes or until stiff peaks form (tips stand straight). Gently fold beaten egg whites into flour mixture, leaving a few fluffs of egg white. (Do not overmix.)

3. Bake waffles in preheated, lightly greased waffle baker according to manufacturer's directions.

4. Serve waffles warm. If you like, serve with Hot Lemon Curd Sauce on the side and dust with powdered sugar. **Makes 12 (2 waffles) servings.**

Hot Lemon Curd Sauce: In a medium saucepan, stir together ½ cup sugar and 1 teaspoon all-purpose flour. Stir in ½ cup water. Cook and stir over medium heat until thickened and bubbly. Remove from heat. Stir half the sugar mixture into 2 lightly beaten egg yolks, blending well. Return egg mixture to the saucepan. Cook, stirring constantly, over medium heat until mixture comes to a gentle boil. Cook and stir for 2 minutes more. Remove from heat. Add 2 tablespoons cut up butter, stirring until melted. Stir in 1 teaspoon finely shredded lemon peel and 3 tablespoons lemon juice. Use sauce immediately or cover surface with plastic wrap until ready to serve.

Per serving: 152 cal, 6 g fat, 51 mg chol, 186 mg sodium, 23 g carbo, 0 g fiber, 2 g pro.

A crisp winter walk through the woods invigorates the mind and body. Be sure to fuel up first with a hearty breakfast.

Swedish Lemon Pancakes

At the Victorian Inn in Abilene, Kansas, sausage or bacon accompanies these lacy pancakes.

PREP 25 minutes   **COOK** 2 minutes per pancake

1½ cups all-purpose flour
　3 tablespoons granulated sugar
　2 teaspoons lemon zest
　½ teaspoon salt
　3 eggs, lightly beaten
2½ cups milk
　1 teaspoon vanilla
　　Butter, melted
　1 cup lemon curd
　　Sweetened Sour Cream (recipe follows)
　　Lingonberry preserves, your favorite jam,
　　　sliced fresh strawberries or raspberries
　　　(optional)
　　Lemon zest
　　Powdered sugar

1. In a medium bowl, combine flour, granulated sugar, 2 teaspoons lemon zest and the salt. In a large bowl, beat the eggs with an electric mixer on medium to high speed for 3 to 5 minutes, until thick and lemon color. Add the milk and vanilla; beat well. Add the flour mixture; beat to make a smooth, thin batter.

2. Use a heat-proof pastry brush to lightly coat a 10-inch nonstick skillet with melted butter. Heat over medium-high heat until water drops dance across the surface. For each pancake, ladle ⅓ cup batter into skillet; lift and tilt skillet to spread batter evenly to make 10-inch-diameter pancakes. Return skillet to heat; cook about 1 minute or until underside is golden brown. Loosen edges with a small spatula. Turn pancake and cook about 1 minute more or until second side is golden brown. Invert onto paper towels. Transfer to a plate; keep warm. Repeat with remaining batter, buttering skillet as needed and reducing heat if necessary.

3. To serve, fold pancakes in half. Spread about 1 tablespoon of lemon curd on one half of the folded pancake. Fold in half again. Serve with Sweetened Sour Cream and, if you like, lingonberry preserves. Sprinkle with lemon zest and powdered sugar. **Makes 8 (2 pancakes) servings.**

Sweetened Sour Cream: Beat 1 cup whipping cream, ½ cup sour cream and 2 tablespoons packed brown sugar with an electric mixer on medium speed until soft peaks form. Do not overbeat.

Per serving: 473 cal, 22 g fat, 161 mg chol, 286 mg sodium, 63 g carbo, 5 g fiber, 8 g pro.

Lingonberries taste like cranberries. They grow in wild profusion in Scandinavian forests. The tart-sweet jam made from lingonberries is a must with lace-thin Swedish pancakes—and it's pretty good with Swedish meatballs, too.

Mini Egg Pastries with Béarnaise Sauce

Cold Spring Inn in Hubertus, Wisconsin, serves these pastries with fresh fruit and cinnamon rolls.

PREP 40 minutes **BAKE** 15 minutes **STAND** 15 minutes

    1 15-ounce package (2 crusts) rolled
       refrigerated unbaked piecrust
       Nonstick cooking spray
    1 tablespoon coarse-ground mustard
    8 ounces thick-sliced bacon, crisp-cooked,
       drained and crumbled
   12 eggs
       Salt and freshly ground black pepper
 1½   cups shredded cheddar cheese (6 ounces)
       Béarnaise Sauce (recipe follows) or your
       favorite hollandaise sauce

1. Let piecrusts stand at room temperature 15 minutes.

2. Unroll piecrusts on a lightly floured surface. Roll from center to edges into 12-inch diameter circles. Cut six 4½- to 5-inch rounds from each piecrust (if necessary, reroll scraps). Press rounds into twelve 2½-inch muffin cups lightly coated with cooking spray.

3. Brush some of the mustard onto the bottom of each round. Top with bacon. Break one egg into a glass measuring cup, taking care not to break the yolk. Hold the lip of the cup as close as possible to the muffin cup and slip egg into the cup over the bacon; repeat with remaining eggs. Top each with salt, pepper and 2 tablespoons of the cheese.

4. Bake in a 350° oven for 15 to 20 minutes or until the eggs are set, the whites are opaque and crust is lightly browned. Remove from oven. Serve each topped with a spoonful of Béarnaise Sauce.

Makes 12 servings.

Béarnaise Sauce: In a small saucepan, combine ¼ cup dry white wine; ¼ cup dry vermouth, champagne vinegar or white wine vinegar; 1 large shallot, finely chopped; 2 tablespoons fresh tarragon; ¼ teaspoon salt; and ⅛ teaspoon white pepper. Bring to boiling; boil, uncovered, about 2 to 4 minutes or until reduced by about half (measure ¼ cup). Remove from heat. Cool for 5 minutes. Pour mixture through a fine-mesh sieve into a small bowl, pressing solids with the back of a spoon. Discard solids. You should have 2 tablespoons strained wine mixture; if less, add enough water to make 2 tablespoons. In the top of a double boiler, combine wine mixture, 4 lightly beaten egg yolks and 1 tablespoon water. Cut ½ cup butter into 2-tablespoon-size pieces; add one to the double boiler. Cook, stirring rapidly with a whisk, until butter melts and sauce begins to thicken. Add the remaining butter, a piece at a time, stirring constantly until melted. Continue to cook and stir for 2 to 3 minutes more or until sauce is thickened. Remove from heat. If sauce is too thick or curdles, whisk in 1 to 2 tablespoons hot water. If you like, strain sauce. Stir in ½ teaspoon snipped fresh Italian (flat-leaf) parsley, ½ teaspoon lemon juice and ¼ teaspoon snipped fresh tarragon or chervil. Season with additional sea salt and white pepper. To keep sauce warm until ready to serve, place in a glass measuring cup in a pan of gently simmering water.

Per serving: 466 cal, 34 g fat, 302 mg chol, 834 mg sodium, 17 g carbo, 0 g fiber, 18 g pro.

Pork 'n' Pippins Quiche

Serve this tasty quiche with seasoned, broiled tomato halves. When you add the apple mixture to the potatoes and sausage, make sure to mix any extra liquid right in with the apples.

PREP 30 minutes **COOK** 18 minutes **BAKE** 50 minutes **STAND** 10 minutes

½ of a 15-ounce package (1 crust) rolled refrigerated unbaked piecrust or 1 homemade unbaked pastry shell
2 medium red potatoes, peeled and cut into ½-inch cubes (about 2 cups)
½ cup apple cider or apple juice
1½ cups thinly sliced peeled Pippin, Granny Smith or other tart apples
1 tablespoon packed brown sugar
¼ teaspoon ground cinnamon
8 ounces bulk pork or turkey sausage, cooked and drained
¼ cup shredded cheddar cheese (1 ounce)
7 eggs, lightly beaten
¼ teaspoon salt
⅛ teaspoon ground black pepper
Sour cream

1. Line a 9-inch pie plate with pastry; flute edge as desired. Line pastry with double thickness of foil. Bake in a 450° oven for 8 minutes; remove foil. Bake for 6 to 8 minutes more or until golden. Remove from oven. Reduce temperature to 325°.

2. Meanwhile, in a medium saucepan, add potatoes and enough water to cover. Bring to boiling; reduce heat. Simmer, covered, for 10 to 12 minutes or until just tender. Drain well; set aside.

3. Meanwhile, in another medium saucepan, bring apple cider to boiling; reduce heat. Add sliced apples, brown sugar and cinnamon. Simmer, uncovered, over medium heat for 8 to 10 minutes or until apple slices are soft and juice is slightly thickened, stirring occasionally.

4. In a large bowl, combine potatoes, apple mixture and sausage. Spoon potato mixture into the hot prebaked pastry shell; top with cheese. In a medium bowl, combine eggs, salt and pepper. Pour over potato mixture in pastry shell. To prevent overbrowning, cover edge of pie with foil.

5. Bake for 50 to 55 minutes or until a knife inserted in center comes out clean. Let stand 10 minutes before serving. Serve with sour cream. **Makes 6 servings.**

Per serving: 460 cal, 29 g fat, 259 mg chol, 686 mg sodium, 30 g carbo, 1 g fiber, 16 g pro.

Traditions for holiday rituals, decorating and food—whether they are long-standing and spring from your ethnic heritage or have been established and maintained by your own kin—build closeness and connections with family and friends.

SMOKED SALMON AND ROASTED PEPPER FRITTATA

WINTER BREAKFAST FRUIT CRUNCH

Smoked Salmon and Roasted Pepper Frittata

Veggies and low-fat cottage cheese stretch the eggs in this frittata. A little salmon or ham boosts the flavor.

PREP 15 minutes **COOK** 10 minutes
BROIL 2 minutes **STAND** 1 minute

	Nonstick cooking spray
½	cup chopped red onion
2	cloves garlic, minced
4	cups baby spinach or torn spinach
8	eggs, lightly beaten, or 2 cups refrigerated or frozen egg product, thawed
¾	cup low-fat cottage cheese or crumbled reduced-fat feta cheese
1	teaspoon herbes de Provence or Italian seasoning, crushed
¼	teaspoon freshly ground black pepper
½	cup chopped bottled roasted red sweet peppers, drained
1	ounce thinly sliced smoked salmon (lox-style), smoked turkey or low-fat reduced-sodium cooked boneless ham, chopped

1. Preheat broiler. Coat an unheated well-seasoned cast-iron or broiler-safe nonstick 10-inch skillet with nonstick spray. Preheat skillet over medium heat. Add onion and garlic. Cook 4 minutes over medium heat or until onion is just tender, stirring occasionally. Stir in spinach; cook 1 minute or until wilted.

2. In a bowl, mix eggs, cottage cheese, herb and pepper. Pour over vegetables in skillet. Cook over medium heat. As mixture sets, run spatula around edge of skillet, lifting egg so uncooked portion flows underneath. Continue cooking and lifting edges until almost set. Sprinkle sweet peppers and salmon on top.

3. Broil 4 to 5 inches from heat about 2 minutes or until the top is just set. Remove skillet from oven. Let stand for 1 minute before serving. **Makes 6 servings.**

Per serving: 141 cal, 7 g fat, 284 mg chol, 333 mg sodium, 5 g carbo, 1 g fiber, 14 g pro.

Winter Breakfast Fruit Crunch

There are actually fresh fruits that are at peak season during the winter—most notably citrus fruits such as oranges and grapefruits.

START TO FINISH 25 minutes

  4 cups assorted fresh fruit, such as orange or grapefruit sections, chopped apple or pear, seedless grapes, cubed fresh pineapple, and/or peeled and sliced kiwifruit
  2 6-ounce cartons low-fat vanilla yogurt
  2 tablespoons honey
  ½ cup low-fat granola or Grape Nuts cereal (wheat-barley nugget cereal)
  ¼ cup coconut, toasted (optional)

1. Divide fruit among six parfait glasses or individual dishes.

2. Top with yogurt and drizzle with honey. Sprinkle with granola and, if you like, coconut. **Makes 6 servings.**

Per serving: 160 cal, 1 g fat, 3 mg chol, 58 mg sodium, 35 g carbo, 3 g fiber, 4 g pro.

Fruit and Nut Granola

Good choices for dried fruits include raisins, cherries, cranberries or snipped apricots.

PREP 15 minutes **BAKE** 15 minutes

  2 cups regular rolled oats
  ½ cup coarsely chopped pecans or slivered almonds
  ⅓ cup packed brown sugar
  1 teaspoon ground cinnamon
    Dash ground allspice or nutmeg
    Dash salt
  ¼ cup butter
  2 tablespoons honey
  ½ cup dried fruit of choice (optional)

1. In a large bowl, combine oats, pecans, brown sugar, spices and salt; set aside.

2. In a saucepan, melt butter and honey over medium heat, stirring occasionally. Pour over the oat mixture; toss to coat. Spread in a 15x10x1-inch baking pan.

3. Bake in a 300° oven 15 to 20 minutes, stirring after 10 minutes. Remove from oven. If you like, stir in dried fruit.

4. Cool granola completely in pan. Store in an airtight container at room temperature for up to 5 days or freeze for up to 2 months. **Makes 8 servings.**

Per serving: 326 cal, 13 g fat, 15 mg chol, 81 mg sodium, 47 g carbo, 6 g fiber, 8 g pro.

Snowflake-laden birch trees, velvet ribbons and twinkling lights festoon a floral shop in Cedarburg, Wisconsin on one of the Five Festive Friday Eves held between Thanksgiving and Christmas each year.

Cardamom Braid

This Swedish holiday bread comes from Bishop Hill Bakery and Eatery in Illinois.

PREP 20 minutes **RISE** 2 hours **BAKE** 25 minutes **STAND** 20 minutes

1 package active dry yeast
1 teaspoon sugar
¼ cup warm water (105° to 115°)
¾ cup warm milk (105° to 115°)
½ cup sugar
¼ cup butter, melted and cooled
2 tablespoons vegetable oil
1 tablespoon orange zest
¾ teaspoon ground cardamom
½ teaspoon salt
3½ to 4 cups all-purpose flour
    Coarse granulated sugar

1. In a small mixing bowl, dissolve yeast and 1 teaspoon sugar in the warm water; set aside for 10 minutes.

2. In a large mixing bowl, combine the milk, ½ cup sugar, the butter, oil, orange zest, cardamom and salt. Beat with an electric mixer on low to medium speed until combined. Stir in 1 cup of the flour. Add the yeast mixture. Beat on low to medium speed for 30 seconds, scraping bowl constantly. Beat on high speed for 3 minutes. Stir in 2 cups flour, 1 cup at a time. (The dough should be slightly wet.) Cover; let dough rest for 10 minutes.

3. Knead on a lightly floured surface, working in enough remaining flour to make a moderately soft, smooth and elastic dough (3 to 5 minutes). Shape into a ball. Place in a greased bowl, turning once to grease surface. Cover; let rise in a warm place until doubled in size (1 to 1¼ hours).

4. Punch dough. Turn onto a floured surface. Cover; let rest for 10 minutes.

5. Divide dough into thirds and shape into 14-inch-long ropes. Place the ropes 1 inch apart on a lightly greased baking sheet. Starting in the middle, loosely braid to each end. Pinch ends to seal and tuck under the loaf. Cover; let rise in a warm place until nearly doubled (about 1 hour).

6. Lightly brush or mist top of braids with water; sprinkle with coarse sugar.

7. Bake in a 375° oven for 25 to 30 minutes or until bread sounds hollow when you tap the top. (Internal temperature should be 180°.) If necessary to prevent overbrowning, cover loosely with foil for the last 10 minutes of baking. Remove from baking sheet. Cool on a wire rack. **Makes 10 to 12 servings.**

Per serving: 282 cal, 8 g fat, 14 mg chol, 167 mg sodium, 47 g carbo, 1 g fiber, 5 g pro.

Swedish Tea Ring

The recipe for this indulgent bread comes from the Midwest Living® Culinary and Craft School at Silver Dollar City in Branson, Missouri.

PREP 35 minutes **RISE** 1 hour 30 minutes **BAKE** 25 minutes **STAND** 20 minutes

1 tablespoon active dry yeast
¼ cup warm water (105° to 115°)
1 cup warm skim milk (105° to 115°)
5 to 5½ cups all-purpose flour
¼ cup granulated sugar
1 teaspoon salt
1 cup cold butter, cut into ½-inch pieces
4 egg yolks, lightly beaten
1 cup chopped walnuts or pecans
1 cup packed brown sugar
½ cup butter, softened
4½ teaspoons ground cinnamon
Powdered Sugar Glaze (recipe follows)
Chopped walnuts or pecans, toasted
Red and/or green candied cherries

1. In a small mixing bowl, dissolve the yeast in the warm water; set aside for 10 minutes. Add warm milk; set aside.

2. In a large mixing bowl, combine 3 cups of flour, the sugar and salt. Use a pastry blender or a stand mixer fitted with a dough hook to cut the 1 cup cold butter into the flour mixture until pieces are pea size. Add milk mixture and egg yolks to flour mixture. Beat with an electric mixer on low to medium speed for 30 seconds. Scrape bowl and beat on high speed for 3 minutes more. Stir in as much of the remaining flour as you can.

3. Turn the dough out onto a lightly floured surface. Knead in enough of the remaining flour to make a moderately soft, smooth and elastic dough (3 to 5 minutes). Shape dough into a ball. Place in a lightly greased bowl, turning once to grease the surface. Cover and let rise in a warm place until doubled (1 to 1½ hours). (Or cover bowl with plastic wrap and store dough in the refrigerator overnight.)

4. Punch dough. Turn out onto a floured surface. Cover; let rest for 10 minutes.

5. For filling: In a small mixing bowl, combine 1 cup walnuts, the brown sugar, ½ cup softened butter and the cinnamon. Set aside.

6. Roll dough into a 20x12-inch rectangle*. Spread filling over dough, leaving 1 inch unfilled along the long sides. Loosely roll up rectangle, starting at a long side. Moisten edges; pinch firmly to seal. Place dough roll, seam side down, on a very large baking sheet lined with parchment paper. Bring ends together to form a ring. Moisten ends; pinch together to seal ring. Flatten slightly.

7. Using a sharp knife, cut slices from outside edge to center at 1½-inch intervals around ring, leaving 1 inch attached at center. Gently turn each slice cut side down. Cover; let rise in a warm place until nearly doubled (30 to 40 minutes; 3 hours for chilled dough**).

8. Bake in a 350° oven for 25 to 30 minutes or until ring sounds hollow when you tap the top. (The center will be lighter, and the filling may have leaked.) If necessary to prevent overbrowning, cover ring with foil for the last 5 to 10 minutes of baking. Remove from baking sheet; cool on a wire rack. Spoon Powdered Sugar Glaze over ring and sprinkle with toasted nuts and candied cherries. **Makes 16 to 20 servings.**

Powdered Sugar Glaze: In a small mixing bowl, combine 1 cup powdered sugar, 1 tablespoon milk, 1 teaspoon butter flavoring and 1 teaspoon vanilla. Add milk to make a glaze of drizzling consistency.

*Tip: For two smaller rings, divide dough in half. Roll each half into a 12x10-inch rectangle. Divide the filling between the two rectangles. Roll as directed; place rings on separate baking sheets lined with parchment paper. Let rise and bake as above. Makes 8 to 10 servings per loaf.

**Tip: Put dough in an oven preheated to 200° and turned off. It will rise in about half the time indicated.

Per serving: 483 cal, 25 g fat, 92 mg chol, 312 mg sodium, 59 g carbo, 2 g fiber, 7 g pro.

HUDSON BAY
BREAD

Hudson Bay Bread

Think of this chewy, honey-flavor snack from Gunflint Lodge in Grand Marais, Minnesota, as a hearty homemade energy bar. Slices are traditionally served with peanut butter spread on top for a boost of filling protein.

PREP 15 minutes **BAKE** 22 minutes
COOL 10 minutes

  2 cups butter or margarine, softened
1½ cups sugar
  ⅓ cup honey
  3 tablespoons cornstarch
  3 tablespoons light-color corn syrup
10 cups regular rolled oats

1. In a very large mixing bowl, beat softened butter with an electric mixer on medium to high speed for 30 seconds. Add sugar and beat until combined. Beat in honey, cornstarch and corn syrup until combined. Gradually stir in oats. (Dough will be crumbly.)

2. Press firmly into a 15x10x1-inch baking pan. Bake in a 375° oven for 22 to 24 minutes, rotating pan once, until top is light brown and has tiny bubbles across the entire surface. Do not overbake. Cool in pan 10 minutes. Cut into 24 pieces. Cool completely. **Makes 24 servings.**

Per serving: 335 cal, 18 g fat, 41 mg chol, 137 mg sodium, 42 g carbo, 3 g fiber, 4 g pro.

Jolly Gin Fizz

This effervescent, gingery cocktail, sweetened with pomegranate juice and spiked with gin, goes down easily!

START TO FINISH 10 minutes

  Ice cubes
6 ounces gin
4 ounces 100% pomegranate juice, chilled
2 ounces fresh-squeezed lime juice
1 12-ounce bottle nonalcoholic ginger beer, chilled
  Lime wedges

1. Fill a cocktail shaker three-quarters full of ice. Add gin, pomegranate juice and lime juice. Cover and shake until cold, about 20 seconds.

2. Strain gin mixture into four 10- to 12-ounce glasses filled with ice while pouring in an equal amount of ginger beer. Garnish with lime wedges. **Makes 4 servings.**

Per serving: 157 cal, O g fat, O mg chol, 9 mg sodium, 16 g carbo, 1 g fiber, O g pro.

A festive door wreath made from apples, limes, evergreens, pine cones, fresh bay leaves and berries welcomes holiday visitors with color and fragrance.

Hot Holiday Apple Cider

This festive drink makes a lovely accompaniment to Christmas cookies.

PREP 10 minutes **COOK** 10 minutes

    1 teaspoon whole cloves
    1 small orange, halved
    8 cups apple cider or apple juice
    4 cups cranberry juice
    1 tablespoon honey
    6 inches stick cinnamon

1. Push tips of cloves into orange rinds.

2. In a Dutch oven, combine cider, juice, honey, cinnamon and clove-studded orange halves. Bring to boiling; reduce heat. Simmer, covered, for 10 minutes. Discard cinnamon and orange before serving. **Makes 12 (1 cup) servings.**

Per serving: 118 cal, 0 g fat, 0 mg chol, 2 mg sodium, 16 g carbo, 0 g fiber, 0 g pro.

Pumpkin Bread

Burchell's White Hill Farmhouse Inn in Minden, Nebraska, grows heirloom Native American produce, including watermelons, pumpkins and squash grown by the Arikara, Omaha and Pawnee. Using their own pumpkins, they have perfected this moist, lightly spiced fall classic. For convenience, you can use canned pumpkin in this simple, old-fashioned recipe.

PREP 25 minutes **BAKE** 55 minutes **COOL** 10 minutes **STAND** overnight

    2½ cups sugar
    ⅔ cup vegetable oil
    4 eggs
    3 cups all-purpose flour
    1½ teaspoons baking soda
    1 teaspoon baking powder
    1 teaspoon salt
    1 teaspoon ground cinnamon
    ½ teaspoon ground ginger
    ¼ teaspoon ground cloves
    ⅔ cup water
    1 15-ounce can pumpkin
    ¾ cup raisins (optional)
    ¾ cup chopped walnuts or pecans (optional)

1. Grease the bottom and ½ inch up sides of two 9x5x3-inch, three 8x4x2-inch or four 7½x3½x2-inch loaf pans; set aside. In a large mixing bowl, beat sugar and oil with an electric mixer on medium speed. Add eggs and beat well; set aside.

2. In a medium bowl, combine flour, baking soda, baking powder, salt, cinnamon, ginger and cloves. Alternately add flour mixture and the water to sugar mixture, beating on low speed after each addition just until combined. Beat in pumpkin. If you like, stir in raisins and walnuts. Spoon batter into prepared pans.

3. Bake in a 375° oven for 55 to 60 minutes for the 9x5-inch loaves, 40 to 45 minutes for the 8x4-inch loaves, or 35 to 40 minutes for the 7½x3½-inch loaves or until a wooden toothpick inserted near centers comes out clean. Cool in pans on wire racks for 10 minutes. Remove from pans. Cool completely on wire racks. Wrap and store overnight before slicing. **Makes 32 servings.**

Per serving: 158 cal, 5 g fat, 24 mg chol, 157 mg sodium, 26 g carbo, 1 g fiber, 2 g pro.

Welcome holiday guests to your home with something sweet to nibble and something warm and spiced to sip.

**HOT HOLIDAY
APPLE CIDER**

PUMPKIN BREAD

**WASABI ALMONDS
AND POPCORN**

**CHEESY TOMATO
SNACK MIX**

Wasabi Almonds and Popcorn

To trim some fat from this recipe, trade the melted butter for five sprays of butter-flavor nonstick spray.

START TO FINISH 15 minutes

- 6 cups air-popped popcorn (unsalted)
- 4 ounces Blue Diamond Bold Wasabi and Soy Sauce Almonds or other Asian-flavor nuts, coarsely chopped
- 1 cup sesame sticks or sesame oat bran sticks
- 2 tablespoons butter or margarine
- ¼ teaspoon garlic powder
- ¼ teaspoon onion powder
- ¼ teaspoon curry powder (optional)

1. In a large bowl, combine popcorn, almonds and sesame sticks.

2. In a microwave-safe glass measuring cup, microwave butter, uncovered, on 100% power (high) about 30 seconds or until melted. Stir in garlic powder, onion powder and, if you like, curry powder. Drizzle butter mixture over popcorn mixture; toss well to coat and serve immediately. **Makes 8 (1 cup) servings.**

Make-ahead directions: Store unbuttered popcorn mixture in a resealable plastic bag or airtight container at room temperature up to 1 day. Add butter mixture before serving.

Per serving: 113 cal, 8 g fat, 5 mg chol, 116 mg sodium, 9 g carbo, 2 g fiber, 3 g pro.

Cheesy Tomato Snack Mix

PREP 15 minutes **BAKE** 30 minutes

- 3 cups bite-size square corn cereal, puffed corn cereal or oyster crackers
- 3 cups bite-size square rice cereal or 3 plain rice cakes, broken into bite-size pieces
- 3 cups bite-size square wheat cereal or round toasted oat cereal
- 1 cup salted roasted soy nuts or corn nuts
- 1 cup small fat-free pretzel knots, circles or bite-size pretzel snaps
- 1 cup fish-shape cheddar cheese crackers
- ¼ cup olive oil or canola oil
- 2 tablespoons dried Italian seasoning, crushed
- 2 tablespoons grated Parmesan cheese
- 2 tablespoons finely snipped dried tomatoes (not oil-packed)
- 1 tablespoon reduced-sodium Worcestershire sauce
- ¼ teaspoon freshly ground black pepper

1. In a large roasting pan, combine the cereals, soy nuts, pretzels and crackers; set aside.

2. In a small bowl, combine oil, Italian seasoning, Parmesan cheese, tomatoes, Worcestershire sauce and pepper. Pour oil mixture over cereal mixture in pan; toss until well coated.

3. Bake, uncovered, in a 300° oven for 30 minutes, stirring twice during baking. Spread snack mix on a large sheet of foil to cool. Store in an airtight container for up to 2 weeks. **Makes 24 (½ cup) servings.**

Per serving: 102 cal, 4 g fat, 1 mg chol, 205 mg sodium, 15 g carbo, 2 g fiber, 3 g pro.

Pick-a-Topper Appetizer Flatbread

Little slices ... big flavor. These flatbread appetizers come loaded with possibilities sure to satisfy everyone at your Super Bowl party or other winter gatherings. Start with a batch of dough, then try one of the topper ideas or use them as inspiration for your own creations.

PREP 45 minutes and 10+ minutes per topper **RISE** 45 minutes **STAND** 10 minutes **BAKE** 10 minutes

1¼ cups warm water (105° to 115°)
2 tablespoons olive oil
1 package active dry yeast
1 teaspoon sugar
3¼ to 3½ cups all-purpose flour
1 teaspoon salt
    Desired toppers (recipes follow; each
        makes enough to top 1 flatbread)
    Cornmeal

1. In a medium bowl, stir together the warm water, olive oil, yeast and sugar; stir to dissolve yeast. Let mixture stand 10 minutes or until foamy.

2. Meanwhile, in a large bowl, stir together 2¾ cups of the flour and the salt. Stir yeast mixture into flour mixture until combined. Stir in as much of remaining flour as you can.

3. Turn dough out onto a lightly floured surface. Knead in enough of the remaining flour to make a soft dough that is smooth and elastic (3 to 5 minutes).

4. Place dough in an oiled bowl, turning once to grease surface of dough. Cover and let rise in a warm place until double in size (45 to 60 minutes).

5. Punch down dough. Turn out dough onto a lightly floured surface. Divide dough into nine equal portions. Cover and let rest for 10 minutes. Roll each portion into a 4x9-inch oval. (Cover remaining dough while working so it does not dry out.)

6. Sprinkle a baking sheet with cornmeal. Place three of the ovals on prepared baking sheet. Top each oval with a topper. Bake in a 450° oven about 10 minutes or until golden. Repeat with the remaining dough ovals. **Makes 9 flatbreads.**

Sweet Potato & Sage: Brush dough with 2 teaspoons olive oil. Top with 5 or 6 thin slices sweet potato, 2 teaspoons snipped fresh sage and 2 teaspoons maple syrup. Sprinkle with 1 tablespoon crumbled, crisp-cooked pancetta. If you like, sprinkle with sea salt and black pepper.

Blue Cheese & Pear: In a medium skillet, cook ½ cup thinly sliced sweet onion in 1 tablespoon hot vegetable oil over medium-low heat until tender and golden brown. Spread onion on dough. Top with 5 to 6 slices thinly sliced pear and sprinkle with 2 tablespoons blue cheese.

Sausage & Green Olive: Spread 2 tablespoons pizza sauce on dough. Top with 2 tablespoons cooked Italian sausage, 1 tablespoon sliced green olives and 2 tablespoons shredded mozzarella cheese.

Barbecue Chicken: Spread 2 tablespoons bottled barbecue sauce on dough. Top with ¼ cup shredded cooked chicken and 1 tablespoon chopped green sweet pepper. Sprinkle with 2 tablespoons shredded Monterey Jack cheese.

Thai Peanut Chicken: Combine ¼ cup shredded cooked chicken, 2 tablespoons bottled peanut sauce and 1 tablespoon shredded carrot. Spoon chicken mixture over dough. Sprinkle with a bias-sliced green onion.

Rosemary & Potato: Sprinkle dough with 2 tablespoons shredded Gruyère cheese. Top with 5 to 6 slices cooked red-skinned potato. Sprinkle with ½ teaspoon snipped fresh rosemary, some sea salt and a few grinds black pepper. Drizzle with 1 to 2 teaspoons olive oil.

Chutney & Grape & Pistachio: Spread 2 tablespoons chutney on dough. Top with 10 halved seedless red grapes and 1 tablespoon coarsely chopped pistachios.

Balsamic & Cremini & Goat Cheese: In a medium skillet, cook ½ cup sliced cremini mushrooms in 2 teaspoons hot vegetable oil until nearly tender. Add 1 tablespoon balsamic vinegar; continue cooking until liquid evaporates and mushrooms are tender. Spread mushrooms over a dough oval. Sprinkle with 2 tablespoons crumbled goat cheese and ½ teaspoon fresh thyme. Just before serving, drizzle with 1 teaspoon balsamic vinegar.

BLUE CHEESE
& PEAR

BARBECUE
CHICKEN

SWEET POTATO
& SAGE

SAUSAGE &
GREEN OLIVE

THAI PEANUT
CHICKEN

CHUTNEY & GRAPE
& PISTACHIO

ROSEMARY
& POTATO

BALSAMIC & CREMINI
& GOAT CHEESE

For generations—83 years, to be exact—Kansas Citians have gathered at Country Club Plaza on Thanksgiving night to watch the holiday lights flick on, a decorating touch that lends even more romance to the beautiful Spanish-inspired architecture of this 15-block mecca of shopping and dining.

Spiced Pumpkin Bisque

The Inn at Irish Hollow in Galena, Illinois, sometimes serves this creamy soup in roasted pie pumpkins.*

PREP 15 minutes **COOK** 45 minutes **STAND** (if making crème fraîche) 2 hours

1 cup whipping cream
2 tablespoons buttermilk
1½ cups chopped onion
4 cloves garlic, minced
¼ cup butter
1½ teaspoons curry powder
¼ to ½ teaspoon cayenne pepper
½ teaspoon salt
½ teaspoon ground coriander
3 cups chicken or vegetable broth
1 15-ounce can pumpkin
1 cup half-and-half or light cream
Chopped fresh Italian (flat-leaf) parsley, chives and/or dill

1. For crème fraîche: In a screw-top jar, combine whipping cream and buttermilk. Cover and shake well. Let stand at room temperature for 2 to 5 hours or until thickened. Store in refrigerator for up to 3 weeks. (Or use purchased crème fraîche, available in large supermarkets.)

2. For soup: Cook onion and garlic in hot butter in a large saucepan over medium heat until tender, about 5 minutes, stirring occasionally. Add curry powder, cayenne, salt and coriander. Cook and stir for 5 minutes more. Add chicken broth. Bring to boiling; reduce heat. Simmer, uncovered, for 25 minutes.

3. Stir pumpkin and half-and-half into the onion mixture. Cook, uncovered, over medium to medium-low heat about 10 minutes or until heated through. (Do not boil.) Cool mixture slightly.

4. Using a handheld immersion blender, blend soup mixture until nearly smooth; heat through before serving. (Or let soup cool slightly. Transfer mixture, one-third at a time, to a blender or food processor. Cover and blend or process until smooth. Return soup to saucepan; heat through before serving.)

5. Top each serving with crème fraîche and parsley. **Makes 8 (¾ cup) servings.**

*Tip: Serve the pumpkin bisque in roasted pumpkins. Wash and dry small pie pumpkins. Cut off tops, clean out insides, and place on a large cookie sheet. Roast in a 375° oven for 40 minutes. Fill with soup and garnish.

Per serving: 233 cal, 21 g fat, 70 mg chol, 551 mg sodium, 11 g carbo, 2 g fiber, 3 g pro.

During the holiday season, warming one-pot dinners and soups that simmer create a special kind of mealtime magic.

ITALIAN-STYLE CHILI

Italian-Style Chili

Intriguing Italian-style seasoning flavors this chili and there's just enough cayenne to add a touch of heat.

PREP 30 minutes **COOK** 2½ hours

2 tablespoons chili powder
1 tablespoon ground cumin
2 teaspoons dried oregano, crushed
1 teaspoon cayenne pepper
1 teaspoon unsweetened cocoa powder
1 tablespoon olive oil
¾ cup chopped green sweet pepper
¾ cup chopped onion
3 cloves garlic, minced
1 pound bulk Italian sausage
1 pound ground beef
2 tablespoons balsamic vinegar
1 14.5-ounce can diced tomatoes, undrained
1 4.5-ounce can diced green chiles
1 8-ounce can tomato sauce
1 14.5-ounce can Italian-style whole peeled tomatoes in puree, crushed
1 15-ounce can cannellini beans (white kidney beans), rinsed and drained
1 15-ounce can black beans, rinsed and drained
Sour cream (optional)
Shredded cheddar cheese (optional)

1. In a small bowl, mix chili powder, cumin, oregano, cayenne and cocoa powder.

2. In a 4-quart Dutch oven, heat olive oil over medium-high heat. Cook sweet pepper, onion and garlic until tender, stirring frequently so that the garlic does not burn.

3. Meanwhile, in a large skillet, cook the sausage and ground beef until no longer pink; drain. Add half of the spice mixture; mix well. Add meat mixture, vinegar, undrained diced tomatoes, green chiles and tomato sauce to the vegetable mixture in the Dutch oven. Bring to boiling; reduce heat. Simmer, covered, for 2 hours, stirring occasionally.

4. Add the Italian tomatoes, cannellini beans, black beans and remaining spice to the mixture in the Dutch oven. Bring to boiling; reduce heat. Simmer the chili, uncovered, 30 minutes, stirring occasionally. Serve with sour cream and cheese, if you like. **Makes 8 to 10 servings.**

Per serving: 474 cal, 32 g fat, 83 mg chol, 1,057 mg sodium, 26 g carbo, 9 g fiber, 26 g pro.

Red-Hot Whiskey Chili

This simmers 3 hours to mellow the whiskey and beer. Chipotle adds kick.

PREP 30 minutes **COOK** 3 hours

1 pound sliced bacon
1 pound ground beef
2 red and/or green sweet peppers, chopped
1 large red onion, chopped
1½ cups whiskey
2 15- to 16-ounce cans red kidney beans, rinsed and drained
2 12-ounce cans or bottles dark beer
3 cups beef broth
½ to one 11-ounce can chipotle peppers in adobo sauce, snipped
1 6-ounce can tomato paste
¼ cup packed brown sugar
3 tablespoons liquid smoke
3 tablespoons bottled hot sauce
1 teaspoon chili powder
1 teaspoon packaged seasoning mix for chili
Cheese, tortilla chips and/or sour cream (optional)

1. In a 6-quart pot, cook bacon over medium heat until crisp; drain on paper towels. Discard drippings. Chop bacon and return to pot. Add beef, sweet peppers and onion; cook until beef is browned and onion is tender. Drain fat. Remove mixture from pot.

2. Remove pot from heat; add whiskey, stirring to scrape browned bits from pan. Return to heat. Bring to boiling; simmer, uncovered, 5 minutes or until whiskey is reduced slightly. Return bacon and beef mixture to pot. Add beans, beer, broth, peppers in adobo sauce, tomato paste, sugar, liquid smoke, hot sauce, chili powder and chili seasoning. Bring to boiling; reduce heat. Simmer, uncovered, 3 hours; stir occasionally. If you like, top with cheese, chips and/or sour cream. **Makes 10 servings.**

Per serving: 559 cal, 31 g fat, 63 mg chol, 1,209 mg sodium, 29 g carbo, 7 g fiber, 21 g pro.

Texas Heat Chili

Beef tri-tip simmers to a tender finish in this hearty chili.

PREP 25 minutes **COOK** 2 hours

2 pounds beef bottom sirloin steak (tri-tip) or beef chuck roast, cut into ½- to ¾-inch pieces
1 cup chopped onion
1 medium green sweet pepper, chopped
1 clove garlic, minced
2 tablespoons vegetable oil
2 14.5-ounce cans reduced-sodium beef broth
1½ to 2 cups water
2 6-ounce cans low-sodium tomato paste
2 fresh jalapeño peppers, seeded and finely chopped (see note, page 28)
4½ teaspoons chili powder
½ teaspoon crushed red pepper
½ teaspoon dried oregano, crushed
½ teaspoon ground cumin
1 15- to 16-ounce can pinto beans, rinsed and drained

1. In a 4-quart Dutch oven, cook beef, onion, pepper and garlic in oil over medium heat until meat browns; drain fat.

2. Stir remaining ingredients except beans into meat mixture in Dutch oven. Bring to boiling; reduce heat. Simmer, covered, 1½ hours.

3. Stir beans into meat mixture. Simmer, covered, 30 minutes more or until meat is tender. **Makes 6 servings.**

Per serving: 424 cal, 18 g fat, 97 mg chol, 648 mg sodium, 27 g carbo, 8 g fiber, 40 g pro.

Three-Bean Chili

This tomatoey brown-sugar-sauced beef or turkey chili gets great texture from a blend of kidney, black and garbanzo beans.

PREP 25 minutes **COOK** 45 minutes

1 pound ground beef or ground turkey
1 medium green sweet pepper, chopped (¾ cup)
½ cup chopped onion
2 15-ounce cans tomato sauce
1 15½-ounce can red kidney beans, rinsed and drained
1 15-ounce can black beans, rinsed and drained
1 15-ounce can garbanzo beans (chickpeas), rinsed and drained
1 to 3 tablespoons packed brown sugar
1 to 1½ tablespoons chili powder
½ teaspoon salt
¼ teaspoon paprika
1 bay leaf
Salt and ground black pepper
Tortilla chips, dairy sour cream and/or shredded cheddar cheese (optional)

1. In a 4-quart Dutch oven, cook ground beef, green pepper and onion until meat is brown; drain.

2. Stir tomato sauce, kidney beans, black beans, garbanzo beans, brown sugar, chili powder, ½ teaspoon salt, the paprika and bay leaf into meat mixture in Dutch oven. Bring to boiling, reduce heat. Simmer, covered, for 45 minutes.

2. Remove and discard bay leaf. Season chili to taste with salt and black pepper. If you like, serve the chili with tortilla chips, sour cream and/or shredded cheese. **Makes 6 servings.**

Per serving: 433 cal, 17 g fat, 54 mg chol, 1,532 mg sodium, 50 g carbo, 13 g fiber, 28 g pro.

Potluck Chili

Vinegar, sugar, sour cream and bacon give this funky chili a decidedly German touch with a flavor similar to that of baked beans.

PREP 25 minutes **COOK** 30 minutes

1 pound lean ground beef
2 11-ounce cans pork and beans, undrained
1 15- to 16-ounce can red kidney beans, rinsed and drained
1 15- to 16-ounce can butter beans, rinsed and drained
1 14½-ounce can diced tomatoes, undrained
1 8-ounce can tomato sauce
1 cup water
⅓ cup white wine vinegar
2 to 4 tablespoons packed dark brown sugar
¼ cup ketchup
¼ cup molasses
Sour cream
Crisp-cooked bacon

1. In a 4-quart Dutch oven, cook beef until browned; drain off fat.

2. Stir pork and beans, kidney beans, butter beans, diced tomatoes, tomato sauce, the water, vinegar, brown sugar, ketchup and molasses into meat in Dutch oven. Bring to boiling; reduce heat. Simmer, uncovered, about 30 minutes or until slightly thickened.

3. Serve chili topped with sour cream and bacon. **Makes 6 servings.**

Per serving: 478 cal, 13 g fat, 60 mg chol, 1,355 mg sodium, 68 g carbo, 12 g fiber, 32 g pro.

POTLUCK CHILI

PORK CHILI

Pork Chili

PREP 40 minutes ROAST 3 hours BROIL 10 minutes STAND 20 minutes COOK 10 minutes

2 pounds pork shoulder roast (bone-in)
3 tablespoons vegetable oil
2 teaspoons crushed red pepper
1 0.87-ounce envelope pork gravy mix
6 cloves garlic, minced
1 jalapeño chile pepper, halved, seeded and sliced (see note, page 28)
2 Anaheim chile peppers (see note, page 28)
1 poblano chile pepper (see note, page 28)
½ cup chopped onion
3 tablespoons vegetable oil
3 tablespoons all-purpose flour
3 tablespoons chili powder
2 15-ounce cans hominy, undrained
1 14½-ounce can diced tomatoes, undrained
1 14½-ounce can vegetable broth
1 15- to 16-ounce can pinto beans, undrained
1 habañero chile pepper, seeded and minced (see note, page 28)
1 teaspoon dried oregano, crushed
1 teaspoon ground cumin
  Dairy sour cream
  Shredded cheddar cheese

1. Brush all sides of pork with 3 tablespoons oil. Sprinkle with crushed red pepper and gravy mix; rub into meat with fingers. In a roasting pan, combine garlic, jalapeño and 1 cup water. Add meat. Roast, uncovered, in a 350° oven for 3 hours or until pork is tender, adding water as needed to the pan. Remove; cool slightly. When cool enough to handle, shred pork with two forks; set aside. Strain cooking liquid through a fine-mesh strainer; discard solids. Skim fat from liquid; set aside.

2. Preheat broiler. Place Anaheim and poblano peppers on foil-lined baking sheet. Broil 4 to 5 inches from heat 5 minutes per side or until blistered and just starting to char. Remove and wrap in foil. Let stand 20 minutes or until cool enough to handle. Stem and seed peppers. Use a small sharp knife to peel skin from peppers. Chop peppers; set aside.

3. In a 4-quart Dutch oven, cook onion in 3 tablespoons oil until tender. Stir in flour and chili powder until combined. Stir in pork, roasted peppers, undrained hominy, undrained tomatoes, broth, reserved broth from pork, beans, habañero pepper, oregano and cumin. Bring to boiling. Reduce heat; simmer, uncovered, 10 to 20 minutes or until desired consistency. Serve with sour cream and cheese. **Makes 8 servings.**

Per serving: 571 cal, 34 g fat, 92 mg chol, 1,007 mg sodium, 37 g carbo, 8 g fiber, 29 g pro.

Meat Lovers' Chili

There's both beef and pork—and sweet and hot peppers—in this rich chili.

PREP 20 minutes COOK 1 hour 17 minutes

1½ pounds boneless beef chuck roast, cut into 1-inch cubes, or ground beef
1 pound boneless pork loin, cut into 1-inch cubes, or ground pork
2 red or green sweet peppers, chopped
1 large onion, chopped
3 tablespoons vegetable oil
½ cup chopped fresh parsley
4 cloves garlic, minced
1 teaspoon salt
1 small red hot chile pepper, seeded and finely chopped (see note, page 28)
3 14.5-ounce cans stewed tomatoes, cut up and undrained
1 15- to 16-ounce can red kidney beans, rinsed and drained
1 14.5-ounce can beef broth
1 12-ounce can or bottle beer or lager
½ cup melted butter (optional)
¼ cup packed brown sugar
1½ teaspoons ground cumin
1 teaspoon hot pepper sauce (optional)
¾ teaspoon ground black pepper

1. In a 6-quart pot, cook the meat, peppers and onion in hot oil over medium-high heat until meat is browned. Drain mixture if using ground meat. Add the parsley and garlic; cook and stir 2 minutes. Reduce the heat to medium-low. Add the salt and chile pepper; cook, stirring occasionally, 15 minutes more.

2. Stir in undrained tomatoes, beans, broth, beer, butter (if using), brown sugar, cumin, pepper sauce (if using) and black pepper. Bring to boiling; reduce heat. Simmer, uncovered, 1 hour; stir occasionally. **Makes 10 servings.**

Per serving: 381 cal, 18 g fat, 71 mg chol, 798 mg sodium, 25 g carbo, 5 g fiber, 28 g pro.

Chicken and Kielbasa Winter Stew

Deli-roasted chicken makes this hearty, simple soup a snap to prepare.

PREP 30 minutes **COOK** 30 minutes

½ cup chopped onion
½ cup sliced carrot (1 medium)
½ cup sliced celery (1 stalk)
2 cloves garlic, minced
1 tablespoon canola or olive oil
2 14.5-ounce cans chicken broth or 3½ cups
   chicken stock
2 cups cubed potato, parsnip, butternut
   squash and/or sweet potato
1 14.5-ounce can diced tomatoes, undrained
1 8-ounce can tomato sauce
2 teaspoons dried Italian seasoning, crushed
½ teaspoon ground black pepper or
   ¼ teaspoon cayenne pepper
1½ cups bite-size pieces cooked chicken
   (deli-roasted, refrigerated cooked strips
   or leftovers; about 8 ounces)
8 ounces cooked turkey kielbasa, cut into
   ½-inch slices
¼ cup snipped fresh Italian (flat-leaf) parsley

1. In a Dutch oven, cook onion, carrot, celery and garlic in hot oil over medium heat until onion is tender. Add chicken broth, potato, undrained tomatoes, tomato sauce, Italian seasoning and pepper. Bring to boiling; reduce heat. Simmer, covered, for 25 to 30 minutes or until vegetables are tender, stirring occasionally.

2. Stir chicken, kielbasa and parsley into vegetable mixture in Dutch oven. Simmer, covered, about 5 minutes or until heated through. **Makes 6 servings.**

Per serving: 226 cal, 9 g fat, 65 mg chol, 1,431 mg sodium, 19 g carbo, 3 g fiber, 19 g pro.

During the busy holiday season, it's a good idea to have a few recipes in your repertoire that are ready to go when you are. Soups and stews store easily in the refrigerator and only require reheating. These tasty Ham Sliders can be prepped a day ahead.

Ham Sliders

Here's a make-ahead tip: Assemble sliders. Wrap pan in plastic wrap; chill overnight. Add topping and bake the next day.

PREP 15 minutes **BAKE** 20 minutes

¼ cup butter, melted
2 tablespoons all-purpose flour
1 cup pineapple-apricot jam, pineapple jam
   or apricot jam
24 dinner rolls
   Nonstick cooking spray
1½ pounds very thinly sliced cooked ham
12 ounces cheddar cheese, thinly sliced
½ cup butter
¼ cup packed brown sugar
4 teaspoons yellow mustard
2 teaspoons Worcestershire sauce
1 to 1½ teaspoons poppy seeds

1. In a small bowl, combine the melted butter, flour and jam, cutting any large pieces of fruit; set aside.

2. Cut rolls in half and lay bottoms, cut sides up, in an even layer in two 13x9x2-inch baking pans lightly coated with nonstick cooking spray. Spread each roll bottom with 1 teaspoon of jam mixture. Divide ham and cheese among the roll bottoms (about 1 ounce ham and ½ ounce cheese per sandwich). Add roll tops.

3. For topping: In a small saucepan, melt the ½ cup butter over medium heat. Remove from heat; stir in brown sugar, mustard and Worcestershire sauce. Using a pastry brush, coat roll tops with topping. Sprinkle with poppy seeds.

4. Bake in a 350° oven for 20 minutes or until cheese is melted and sliders are heated through. **Makes 24 servings.**

Per serving: 274 cal, 13 g fat, 45 mg chol, 654 mg sodium, 27 g carbo, 1 g fiber, 12 g pro.

HAM SLIDERS

Vegetarian Chili

This vegan chili is beefed up with bulgur and heated up with cayenne.

PREP 30 minutes **COOK** 1 hour 10 minutes

⅓ cup olive oil
2 cups finely chopped onion
2 cups chopped fresh mushrooms
1 cup coarsely chopped carrot
1 cup coarsely chopped green sweet pepper
¾ cup chopped celery
1 tablespoon minced garlic
2 tablespoons chili powder
1 tablespoon ground cumin
1 teaspoon salt
¾ teaspoon dried oregano, crushed
¾ teaspoon dried basil, crushed
½ teaspoon ground black pepper
¼ teaspoon crushed red pepper
2 cups water
2 cups tomato juice
2 cups coarsely chopped tomatoes
¾ cup bulgur
1 15.5-ounce can red kidney beans, undrained
¼ cup dry red wine
3 tablespoons tomato paste
2 tablespoons canned diced green chiles
2 tablespoons lemon juice
1 tablespoon Worcestershire sauce
½ teaspoon bottled hot pepper sauce

1. In a 6-quart Dutch oven, heat olive oil over medium-high heat. Cook and stir onion, mushrooms, carrot, sweet pepper, celery and garlic 3 to 4 minutes or until just tender. Remove from pan.

2. Add chili powder, cumin, salt, oregano, basil, black pepper and crushed red pepper to Dutch oven; cook for 1 to 2 minutes over medium heat until fragrant. Return the cooked vegetable mixture to the Dutch oven and add the water, tomato juice, tomatoes, bulgur, beans, wine, tomato paste, chiles, lemon juice, Worcestershire sauce and hot pepper sauce. Bring to boiling; reduce heat. Simmer, uncovered, 1 hour or until thick. **Makes 6 to 8 servings.**

Per serving: 327 cal, 14 g fat, 0 mg chol, 902 mg sodium, 46 g carbo, 13 g fiber, 11 g pro.

Turkey Chili

PREP 15 minutes **COOK** 20 minutes

1 pound lean ground turkey
2 cups water
1 15- to 16-ounce can red kidney beans, rinsed and drained
1 14.5-ounce can stewed tomatoes, undrained and cut up
1 6-ounce can tomato paste
2 tablespoons chili powder
2 tablespoons dried minced onion
½ teaspoon garlic powder
½ teaspoon dried oregano, crushed
½ teaspoon ground cumin
½ teaspoon paprika
½ teaspoon salt
½ teaspoon ground black pepper
Toppers: sour cream, sliced pitted ripe olives, shredded sharp cheddar cheese and/or chopped green onion (optional)

1. In a large saucepan, brown turkey over medium heat until cooked through, breaking up with the back of a wooden spoon as it cooks. Stir in the water, beans, tomatoes, tomato paste, chili powder, dried onion, garlic powder, oregano, cumin, paprika, salt and ground black pepper. Bring to boiling; reduce heat. Simmer, uncovered, 20 to 30 minutes or until desired consistency, stirring occasionally.

2. If you like, serve bowls of chili with assorted toppers. **Makes 6 servings.**

Per serving: 221 cal, 6 g fat, 53 mg chol, 768 mg sodium, 23 g carbo, 7 g fiber, 23 g pro.

Winter snow and early darkness can't dampen the holiday spirits of Midwesterners. In fact, these hardy and inspired souls use both to their advantage. Glowing lights reflect off of the sparkling snow and welcome visitors inside cozy homes for goodwill and good cheer.

Sweet Potatoes with Pecans and Blue Cheese

PREP 30 minutes **BAKE** 30 minutes

2 large sweet potatoes, peeled and cut lengthwise in thin wedges (1½ pounds)
1 small sweet onion, cut in 1-inch pieces (⅓ cup)
4 tablespoons olive oil
1 tablespoon butter
⅓ cup pecan pieces
1 tablespoon packed light brown sugar
4 teaspoons cider vinegar
1½ teaspoons honey
1 clove garlic, minced (½ teaspoon)
2 tablespoons crumbled blue cheese or finely shredded white cheddar cheese

1. In a 15x10x1-inch baking pan, combine sweet potatoes and onion pieces. Drizzle with 2 tablespoons of the olive oil; sprinkle ½ teaspoon salt and ¼ teaspoon pepper. Toss to combine. Spread in a single layer. Bake in a 375° oven for 30 to 35 minutes or until vegetables are tender, stirring once.

2. Meanwhile, in a small skillet melt butter over medium heat. Stir in pecan pieces, brown sugar and ¼ teaspoon salt. Cook and stir for 2 to 3 minutes or until pecans are coated in the brown sugar mixture. Remove from heat; spread on foil and let stand to cool completely.

3. For dressing: In a small bowl, whisk together vinegar, honey, garlic, ¼ teaspoon salt and ¼ teaspoon pepper. Slowly whisk in remaining 2 tablespoons of the olive oil until combined. Whisk in 1 tablespoon of the blue cheese.

4. To serve, transfer potatoes and onions to serving plate. Drizzle with dressing. Sprinkle with pecans and remaining blue cheese. **Makes 6 side-dish servings.**

Per serving: 241 cal, 16 g fat (3 g sat. fat), 7 mg chol, 487 mg sodium, 23 g carbo, 3 g fiber, 63 g pro.

Butternut Squash and Apple Salad

The dressing for this salad calls for verjus, or pressed unripened grape juice, which has a fruity, slightly acidic taste. Red or white wine vinegar is a good substitute.

PREP 45 minutes **ROAST** 20 minutes

1 pound butternut squash, peeled
3 small firm, tart apples, cored
2 tablespoons butter
2 tablespoons packed brown sugar
2 teaspoons snipped fresh thyme
1 5- to 6-ounce package mixed spring salad greens (about 8 cups)
  Chive Blossom Vinaigrette (recipe follows)
4 ounces Gorgonzola or other blue cheese, coarsely crumbled (1 cup)
  Fresh chive blossoms or snipped fresh chives

1. Cut squash into ½-inch slices, halving and seeding as necessary. Cut apples crosswise into ½-inch slices. Arrange in a shallow, foil-lined baking pan.

2. In a small saucepan, melt butter; stir in brown sugar and thyme. Drizzle or brush over squash and apple.

3. Roast, uncovered, in a 425° oven for 15 minutes. Transfer apple slices to a plate and keep warm. Return pan to oven. Roast squash for 5 to 10 minutes more or until tender. Or grill squash and apple slices in a grill pan until tender, allowing 10 to 12 minutes for squash slices and 5 minutes for apple slices, turning once.

4. To serve, stack the warm squash and apple slices on salad greens. Drizzle with Chive Blossom Verjus Vinaigrette. Sprinkle with cheese and chive blossoms. Serve immediately. **Makes 6 servings.**

Chive Blossom Vinaigrette: In a blender or food processor, combine ½ cup verjus, white wine vinegar or red wine vinegar; 8 fresh chive blossoms or 1 tablespoon snipped fresh chives or sliced green onion; 1 tablespoon honey; 1 clove garlic, halved; ⅛ teaspoon salt; and ⅛ teaspoon freshly ground pepper. Cover and blend or process until combined. With blender or processor running, slowly add 1 cup extra-virgin olive oil in a thin, steady stream (dressing will thicken as oil is added). Season to taste. Refrigerate vinaigrette up to 1 week. Shake well before serving.

Per serving: 526 cal, 45 g fat, 27 mg chol, 350 mg sodium, 26 g carbo, 4 g fiber, 5 g pro.

BUTTERNUT SQUASH AND APPLE SALAD

PAPPA'S PEAR STUFFING

CINNAMON CARROTS WITH MAPLE THYME BUTTER

Pappa's Pear Stuffing

Serve this savory-sweet dressing from the Story Inn in Nashville, Indiana, with roasted or grilled pork or poultry or ham.

PREP 30 minutes **COOL** 10 minutes **BAKE** 40 minutes

2 large white onions, chopped (2 cups)
1 stalk celery with leaves, chopped (½ cup)
¾ cup butter
2 large tart apples, peeled, cored and chopped (about 2 cups)
2 medium pears, peeled, cored and chopped (about 2 cups)
1 6- to 6.5-ounce can or jar sliced mushrooms, drained
12 cups dry bread cubes*
4 eggs, lightly beaten
⅔ cup chicken broth
¼ cup packed brown sugar
1 teaspoon salt
1 teaspoon dried thyme, crushed
½ teaspoon dried sage, crushed
¼ teaspoon ground white pepper
¼ teaspoon ground mace
¼ teaspoon dried marjoram, crushed

1. In a large skillet, cook onions and celery in hot butter until tender. Add apples and pears. Cook for 2 to 4 minutes more, until apples are tender. Remove from heat. Stir in mushrooms.

2. In an extra-large mixing bowl, toss together the bread cubes and onion mixture. Let stand for 10 minutes to cool.

3. In a small bowl, combine remaining ingredients. Drizzle over bread mixture, tossing lightly to combine. If needed, add broth, 2 tablespoons at a time, to moisten mixture. Place in a 13x9x2-inch baking dish or a 3-quart casserole.

4. Bake, covered, in a 375° oven for 20 minutes. Uncover; bake about 20 to 30 minutes more or until top is golden brown and an instant-read thermometer inserted in the center of the stuffing registers 165°. **Makes 10 to 12 servings.**

*To make dry bread cubes: Cut fresh sliced bread into 1-inch cubes. (Eighteen to 20 slices yields 12 cups.) Spread in two 15½x10½x1-inch baking pans. Bake in 300° oven for 15 to 20 minutes or until cubes are dry, turning twice. Cool. Store in an airtight container at room temperature for up to 1 week.

Per serving: 345 cal, 17 g fat, 111 mg chol, 740 mg sodium, 41 g carbo, 4 g fiber, 8 g pro.

Cinnamon Carrots with Maple Thyme Butter

The humble carrot dresses up for the holidays in this recipe from Big Cedar Lodge in Ridgedale, Missouri.

PREP 15 minutes **ROAST** 19 minutes

24 baby carrots with tops (about 1 pound)
1 tablespoon olive oil
3 inches stick cinnamon, broken in half, or ⅛ teaspoon ground cinnamon
Sea salt or kosher salt
3 tablespoons pure maple syrup
2 to 3 teaspoons snipped fresh thyme
1 tablespoon red wine vinegar
¼ teaspoon sea or kosher salt
¼ cup unsalted butter, cut into pieces and softened
Freshly ground black pepper

1. Snip tops from carrots, leaving ½ inch of the greens. Scrub carrots and peel; rinse and dry well.

2. In a shallow roasting pan, toss the carrots with olive oil, cinnamon and a pinch of salt. Spread in an even layer.

3. Roast, uncovered, in a 400° oven for 15 to 20 minutes or just until tender, stirring occasionally.

4. Meanwhile, in a small mixing bowl, combine maple syrup, thyme, vinegar and ¼ teaspoon salt.

5. Remove the carrots from the oven. Add the syrup mixture, butter and a pinch of pepper; toss to coat. Roast for 4 to 5 minutes more, until the carrots are tender and browned. Discard cinnamon pieces, if using. **Makes 4 servings.**

Per serving: 211 cal, 15 g fat, 31 mg chol, 217 mg sodium, 19 g carbo, 3 g fiber, 1 g pro.

Pistachio Cranberry Icebox Cookies

These red- and green-flecked cookies come from the Inn at Cedar Falls in Logan, Ohio.

PREP 25 minutes **CHILL** 2 hours **BAKE** 10 minutes per batch **COOL** 1 minute

¾ cup unsalted butter, softened
⅓ cup granulated sugar
½ teaspoon ground cinnamon
½ teaspoon orange zest
¼ teaspoon salt
1½ cups all-purpose flour
½ cup finely chopped pistachio nuts
⅓ cup snipped dried cranberries
1 egg, lightly beaten
¼ cup coarse white decorating sugar

1. In a large mixing bowl, beat the butter with an electric mixer on medium to high speed for 30 seconds. Add the granulated sugar, cinnamon, orange zest and salt. Beat about 3 minutes or until pale and fluffy, scraping sides of bowl occasionally. Reduce speed to low. Beat in as much of the flour as you can, ½ cup at a time, with the mixer. Stir in any remaining flour. Stir in pistachio nuts and cranberries. Knead dough until smooth. Divide dough in half.

2. On waxed paper, shape each half into an 8½-inch-long log (about 1½ inches across). Lift and smooth the waxed paper to shape the logs. Wrap each log in plastic wrap or waxed paper. Chill about 2 hours or until dough is firm enough to slice.

3. Unwrap dough logs; reshape, if necessary. Brush the beaten egg over sides (but not ends) of each log. Sprinkle coarse white decorating sugar on a separate sheet of parchment or waxed paper. Roll dough logs in sugar, pressing to coat evenly. Reshape, if necessary.

4. Cut logs into ¼-inch-thick slices. Rotate logs while cutting to prevent flattening, freezing briefly if necessary. Place slices 1 inch apart on cookie sheets lined with parchment paper.

5. Bake in a 350° oven for 10 to 12 minutes or until edges are firm and just starting to brown. Cool on cookie sheets for 1 minute. Transfer cookies to wire racks; cool. **Makes about 60 cookies.**

Per cookie: 48 cal, 3 g fat, 9 mg chol, 11 mg sodium, 5 g carbo, 0 g fiber, 1 g pro.

If there is any sort of sweet that is most associated with Christmas, it's the enduring and endearing cookie. The variety of Christmas cookies is stunning which simply means there are more kinds to try.

Oreo Truffles

PREP 20 minutes **FREEZE** 15 minutes
CHILL 30 minutes **STAND** 30 minutes

1 15.35-ounce package chocolate sandwich cookies with white filling
1 8-ounce package cream cheese, softened
1⅔ cups dark chocolate pieces or white baking pieces (10 ounces)
2 tablespoons shortening
⅓ cup white baking pieces or dark chocolate pieces (2 ounces)

1. In a food processor, process one-fourth of the cookies until finely crushed. Transfer to a large mixing bowl. Repeat with remaining cookies.

2. Beat crushed cookies and cream cheese with an electric mixer on low speed until well combined. Shape the mixture into 1-inch balls. Place balls on a baking sheet lined with waxed paper and freeze for 15 minutes or until firm.

3. Meanwhile, in a heavy medium saucepan, melt the 10 ounces of chocolate and the shortening over low heat, stirring until smooth. Remove from heat and cool slightly.

4. Use a fork to dip truffles into chocolate mixture, allowing excess to drip back into saucepan. Place truffles on a baking sheet lined with waxed paper; freeze for a few minutes, or chill in the refrigerator about 30 minutes, until firm.

5. In a heavy small saucepan, melt the ⅓ cup white baking pieces over low heat, stirring until smooth. Place melted chocolate in a resealable plastic bag. Snip a tiny corner of bag and drizzle chocolate over tops of the truffles. Chill for a few minutes until set. Store in refrigerator. Let stand at room temperature for about 30 minutes before serving. **Makes 40 truffles.**

Per truffle: 126 cal, 8 g fat, 7 mg chol, 74 mg sodium, 14 g carbo, 1 g fiber, 1 g pro.

Mystery Cookies

Tomato soup is the secret to these cookies.

PREP 20 minutes **STAND** at least 15 minutes
BAKE 10 minutes per batch

2½ cups all-purpose flour
1 teaspoon baking soda
1 teaspoon ground cinnamon
½ teaspoon salt
½ teaspoon ground nutmeg
½ teaspoon ground allspice
1¾ cups sugar
¼ cup butter, melted
1 egg
½ of a 10.75-ounce can condensed tomato soup (about ½ cup)
½ teaspoon vanilla
1 cup raisins
1 cup chopped walnuts

1. In a medium bowl, combine flour, baking soda and spices; set aside. In a large bowl, combine sugar and melted butter. Let stand for 5 minutes. Beat in egg, tomato soup and vanilla with an electric mixer on medium speed until combined. Beat in as much of the flour mixture as you can. Stir in any remaining flour mixture. Stir in raisins and walnuts. (Dough will be sticky.) Let stand for at least 10 minutes.

2. Drop by rounded tablespoons 2 inches apart onto baking sheets lined with parchment paper.

3. Bake in 350° oven for 10 to 12 minutes or until edges are just light brown. Cool on cookie sheet for 2 minutes. Transfer to wire racks and let cool. **Makes 42 cookies.**

Per cookie: 102 cal, 3 g fat, 7 mg chol, 83 mg sodium, 18 g carbo, 1 g fiber, 2 g pro.

MYSTERY
COOKIES

OREO
TRUFFLES

PISTACHIO
CRANBERRY
ICEBOX
COOKIES

Vienna Almond Cutouts

These cookies taste great on their own, but if you like, decorate them with royal icing. (Recipe pictured on page 180.)

PREP 20 minutes **CHILL** 2 hours
BAKE 8 minutes per batch

¾ cup slivered almonds, toasted
2¼ cups all-purpose flour
¼ teaspoon salt
1 cup butter, softened
¾ cup sugar
1 egg
1 teaspoon vanilla
½ teaspoon lemon zest
¼ teaspoon almond extract (optional)

1. In a food processor, finely grind toasted almonds with on/off pulses. Combine in a small bowl with flour and salt; set aside.

2. Beat butter and sugar on medium speed until light and fluffy. Beat in egg, vanilla, lemon zest and, if you like, almond extract, scraping sides of bowl as needed. Beat in as much of the flour mixture as you can; stir in the rest. Divide dough in half; wrap in plastic. Chill for 2 hours.

3. On a lightly floured surface, roll dough to ¼ inch thickness. Cut desired shapes; chilling and rerolling scraps. Place 1 inch apart on an ungreased cookie sheet.

4. Bake in a 350° oven for 8 to 12 minutes or until edges are light brown and centers are set. Cool for 1 minute before transferring to a wire rack to cool completely. **Makes 48 cookies.**

Per cookie: 77 cal, 5 g fat, 15 mg chol, 41 mg sodium, 8 g carbo, 0 g fiber, 1 g pro.

Cranberry-Orange Cheesecake

This showstopper dessert comes from Big Cedar Lodge in Ridgedale, Missouri.

PREP 40 minutes **BAKE** 68 minutes **COOL** 2 hours 45 minutes **CHILL** overnight

1 9-ounce package chocolate wafer cookies, broken
2 ounces bittersweet or semisweet chocolate, coarsely chopped
5 tablespoons unsalted butter, melted
4 8-ounce packages cream cheese, softened
1½ cups sugar
3 tablespoons all-purpose flour
2 teaspoons orange zest
1 teaspoon vanilla
4 eggs
½ cup sugar
1 teaspoon cornstarch
3 tablespoons water
2 cups fresh cranberries
½ teaspoon orange zest

1. In a food processor, finely grind cookies and chocolate. Add butter; process with on/off turns until clumps form. Press mixture onto the bottom and about 1¼ inches up the sides of a 9-inch springform pan with 2¾-inch-high sides. Bake in a 325° oven about 8 minutes or until set.

2. Remove from oven, and increase oven temperature to 350°. When the crust has cooled, wrap two layers of heavy-duty foil around the bottom and sides of the pan.

3. In an extra-large mixing bowl, beat cream cheese with an electric mixer on medium to high speed until smooth. Add 1½ cups sugar, the flour, 2 teaspoons orange zest and the vanilla. Beat until well combined. Add eggs, one at a time, beating on low speed just until combined.

4. Pour filling into crust-lined pan. Place springform pan in a large roasting pan. (Make sure there is at least 1 inch between springform pan and edges of roasting pan.) Place roasting pan on oven rack. Carefully pour enough hot water into roasting pan to come halfway up the sides of the springform pan.

5. Bake for 60 to 70 minutes or until edge of cheesecake is firm and center appears nearly set when lightly shaken. Remove pan from water bath; transfer to a wire rack and cool 15 minutes. Remove foil. Use a small metal spatula to loosen cheesecake from sides of pan. Cool for 30 minutes more. Remove sides of pan and cool about 2 hours or until completely cooled. Cover with plastic wrap and chill overnight before serving. (Can be stored in refrigerator for up to 2 days.)

6. For cranberry topping: In a medium saucepan, combine ½ cup sugar and the cornstarch. Stir in the water. Cook and stir over medium-low heat until thickened and bubbly. Add cranberries. Bring to boiling; reduce heat. Boil gently, uncovered, over medium-high heat for 3 to 4 minutes or until cranberries pop, stirring occasionally. Stir in the ½ teaspoon orange zest. Cool completely. Cover and chill overnight. (Can be stored in refrigerator for up to 2 days.)

7. To serve, top cheesecake with cranberry topping. **Makes 16 servings.**

Per serving: 441 cal, 28 g fat, 119 mg chol, 311 mg sodium, 44 g carbo, 2 g fiber, 6 g pro.

CRANBERRY-ORANGE
CHEESECAKE

White Chocolate Crème Brûlée

The recipe for these sweet, berry-topped beauties comes from French Lick Springs Hotel in French Lick, Indiana.

PREP 25 minutes **BAKE** 1 hour **CHILL** up to 8 hours **STAND** 30 minutes

2 cups whipping cream
3 ounces white baking chocolate with cocoa butter, chopped
4 egg yolks, lightly beaten
½ cup sugar
½ teaspoon vanilla
¼ cup sugar
Fresh strawberries or raspberries

1. In a heavy medium saucepan, heat and stir ⅓ cup of the whipping cream and the white chocolate over low heat until chocolate is melted. Gradually whisk in remaining whipping cream. Bring to a simmer. Remove from heat.

2. In a large mixing bowl, whisk together egg yolks, ½ cup sugar and the vanilla. Very gradually whisk the cream mixture into the egg yolk mixture.

3. Place six ¾-cup ramekins or 6-ounce custard cups in a 13x9x2-inch (3-quart) baking dish. Divide the custard mixture among the ramekins or custard cups. Set baking dish on the oven rack. Pour enough boiling water or very hot water into the baking dish to reach halfway up the sides of the ramekins.

4. Bake, uncovered, in a 325° oven about 1 hour or until custards are nearly set when gently shaken. Remove ramekins from baking dish; cool on a wire rack. Cover; chill for up to 8 hours.

5. Let stand at room temperature 30 minutes before serving. Sprinkle each with some of the ¼ cup sugar and caramelize with a culinary blowtorch. (Or place the ¼ cup sugar in an 8-inch skillet. Heat over medium-high heat until sugar begins to melt, shaking skillet occasionally to heat sugar evenly. Do not stir. Once sugar starts to melt, reduce heat to low; cook about 3 minutes more or until all the sugar is melted and golden, stirring as needed. Quickly drizzle caramelized sugar over the custards.)

6. Garnish with berries and serve immediately. **Makes 6 servings.**

Per serving: 496 cal, 37 g fat, 233 mg chol, 46 mg sodium, 38 g carbo, 0 g fiber, 5 g pro.

Is there anything sweeter than dessert? Maybe a trio of puppies under the Christmas tree.

Double Chocolate-Espresso Truffle Pie

Save room for a thin slice of this überrich pie after your holiday meal. It's a perfect complement to more traditional fruit or pumpkin pies.

PREP 40 minutes **BAKE** 14 minutes **CHILL** 8 hours

1½ cups all-purpose flour
 3 tablespoons unsweetened cocoa powder
 2 tablespoons packed brown sugar
 ½ teaspoon salt
 ½ cup butter, cut up
 5 tablespoons cold water
 2 cups whipping cream
 6 ounces 60%–70% dark chocolate or bittersweet chocolate, chopped
 1 cup granulated sugar
 6 egg yolks, lightly beaten
 3 tablespoons brewed espresso or strong brewed coffee
 1 teaspoon vanilla
   Sweetened whipped cream
   Chocolate curls and/or shavings (optional)

1. For pastry: In a food processor, combine flour, cocoa powder, brown sugar and salt. Process until just combined. Add butter. Process with on/off turns until butter pieces are pea-size. With processor running, quickly add the water through feed tube until dough just comes together.

2. Gather mixture into a ball, kneading gently until it holds together. Gently pat dough into a disk.

3. On a lightly floured surface, roll dough from center to edges into a 12-inch circle. Wrap around rolling pin; unroll into a 9-inch glass pie plate, easing into pie plate without stretching it. Trim pastry to ½ inch beyond edge of pie plate. Fold under pastry even with edge of plate; crimp as desired. Using a fork, prick bottom and sides of pastry, being sure to prick where bottom and sides meet. Line pastry with a double thickness of foil.

4. Bake in a 450° oven for 8 minutes. Remove foil. Bake for 6 to 8 minutes more or until pastry is set and looks dry. Cool on a wire rack.

5. For filling: In a medium heavy saucepan, combine whipping cream, chocolate and granulated sugar. Cook and stir over medium heat about 10 minutes or until mixture comes to boiling and thickens. If chocolate flecks remain, beat with a wire whisk until fully melted and blended into the cream.

6. Gradually stir half of the hot mixture into egg yolks. Return egg yolk mixture to saucepan. Cook and stir for 2 minutes. Remove from heat; stir in espresso and vanilla. Cool slightly. Pour warm filling into the baked shell. Cover and chill for 8 to 24 hours or until filling is set.

7. Top each serving with whipped cream. If you like, garnish with chocolate curls. **Makes 10 servings.**

Per serving: 579 cal, 41 g fat, 217 mg chol, 229 mg sodium, 49 g carbo, 2 g fiber, 6 g pro.

Most of the year, we try to be good. We eat right and exercise as much as we can. But during the holidays—faced with a wedge of silky mocha-truffle pie—we'll opt for *eating* something good. Really good.

METRIC INFORMATION

The charts on this page provide a guide for converting measurements from the U.S. customary system, which is used throughout this book, to the metric system.

PRODUCT DIFFERENCES

Most of the ingredients called for in the recipes in this book are available in most countries. However, some are known by different names. Here are some common American ingredients and their possible counterparts:

- Sugar (white) is granulated, fine granulated or castor sugar.
- Confectioners' sugar is icing sugar.
- All-purpose flour is enriched, bleached or unbleached white household flour. When self-rising flour is used in place of all-purpose flour in a recipe that calls for leavening, omit the leavening agent (baking soda or baking powder) and salt.
- Light-color corn syrup is golden syrup.
- Cornstarch is cornflour.
- Baking soda is bicarbonate of soda.
- Vanilla or vanilla extract is vanilla essence.
- Green, red or yellow sweet peppers are capsicums or bell peppers.
- Golden raisins are sultanas.

VOLUME AND WEIGHT

The United States traditionally uses cup measures for liquid and solid ingredients. The chart, top right, shows the approximate imperial and metric equivalents. If you are accustomed to weighing solid ingredients, the following approximate equivalents will be helpful.

- 1 cup butter, castor sugar or rice = 8 ounces = ½ pound = 250 grams
- 1 cup flour = 4 ounces = ¼ pound = 125 grams
- 1 cup icing sugar = 5 ounces = 150 grams

Canadian and U.S. volume for a cup measure is 8 fluid ounces (237 ml), but the standard metric equivalent is 250 ml. One British imperial cup is 10 fluid ounces.

In Australia, 1 tablespoon equals 20 ml, and there are 4 teaspoons in the Australian tablespoon.

Spoon measures are used for smaller amounts of ingredients. Although the size of the tablespoon varies slightly in different countries, for practical purposes and for recipes in this book, a straight substitution is all that's necessary. Measurements made using cups or spoons always should be level unless stated otherwise.

COMMON WEIGHT RANGE REPLACEMENTS

Imperial / U.S.	Metric
½ ounce	15 g
1 ounce	25 g or 30 g
4 ounces (¼ pound)	115 g or 125 g
8 ounces (½ pound)	225 g or 250 g
16 ounces (1 pound)	450 g or 500 g
1¼ pounds	625 g
1½ pounds	750 g
2 pounds or 2¼ pounds	1,000 g or 1 Kg

OVEN TEMPERATURE EQUIVALENTS

Fahrenheit Setting	Celsius Setting*	Gas Setting
300°F	150°C	Gas Mark 2 (very low)
325°F	160°C	Gas Mark 3 (low)
350°F	180°C	Gas Mark 4 (moderate)
375°F	190°C	Gas Mark 5 (moderate)
400°F	200°C	Gas Mark 6 (hot)
425°F	220°C	Gas Mark 7 (hot)
450°F	230°C	Gas Mark 8 (very hot)
475°F	240°C	Gas Mark 9 (very hot)
500°F	260°C	Gas Mark 10 (extremely hot)
Broil	Broil	Grill

*Electric and gas ovens may be calibrated using celsius. However, for an electric oven, increase celsius setting 10 to 20 degrees when cooking above 160°C. For convection or forced air ovens (gas or electric) lower the temperature setting 25°F/10°C when cooking at all heat levels.

BAKING PAN SIZES

Imperial / U.S.	Metric
9x1½-inch round cake pan	22- or 23x4-cm (1.5 L)
9x1½-inch pie plate	22- or 23x4-cm (1 L)
8x8x2-inch square cake pan	20x5-cm (2 L)
9x9x2-inch square cake pan	22- or 23x4.5-cm (2.5 L)
11x7x1½-inch baking pan	28x17x4-cm (2 L)
2-quart rectangular baking pan	30x19x4.5-cm (3 L)
13x9x2-inch baking pan	34x22x4.5-cm (3.5 L)
15x10x1-inch jelly roll pan	40x25x2-cm
9x5x3-inch loaf pan	23x13x8-cm (2 L)
2-quart casserole	2 L

U.S. / STANDARD METRIC EQUIVALENTS

⅛ teaspoon = 0.5 ml	⅓ cup = 3 fluid ounces = 75 ml
¼ teaspoon = 1 ml	½ cup = 4 fluid ounces = 125 ml
½ teaspoon = 2 ml	⅔ cup = 5 fluid ounces = 150 ml
1 teaspoon = 5 ml	¾ cup = 6 fluid ounces = 175 ml
1 tablespoon = 15 ml	1 cup = 8 fluid ounces = 250 ml
2 tablespoons = 25 ml	2 cups = 1 pint = 500 ml
¼ cup = 2 fluid ounces = 50 ml	1 quart = 1 litre